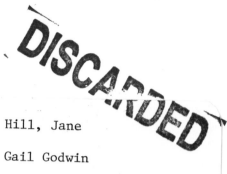
DATE DUE			

Gail Godwin

Twayne's United States Authors Series

Warren French, Editor

University of Wales, Swansea

TUSAS 591

GAIL GODWIN
© *Photo by Jerry Bauer*

Gail Godwin

Jane Hill

Twayne Publishers • New York
Maxwell Macmillan Canada • *Toronto*
Maxwell Macmillan International •
New York Oxford Singapore Sydney

Gail Godwin
Jane Hill

Twayne Publishers   Maxwell Macmillan Canada, Inc.
Macmillan Publishing Company   1200 Eglinton Avenue East
866 Third Avenue   Suite 200
New York, New York 10022   Don Mills, Ontario M3C 3N1

Macmillan Publishing Company is part of the Maxwell Communication
Group of Companies.

Copyediting supervised by Barbara Sutton.
Book design by Barbara Anderson.
Typeset by Graphic Sciences Corp., Cedar Rapids, Iowa.

10 9 8 7 6 5 4 3 2 1

The paper used in this publication meets the minimum requirements
of American National Standard for Information Sciences—Permanence
of Paper for Printed Library Materials, ANSI Z39.48-1984. $\textcircled{\infty}$™

Printed and bound in the United States of America.

Library of Congress Cataloging-in-Publication Data

Hill, Jane.
    Gail Godwin / Jane Hill.
        p. cm. — (Twayne's United States authors series ; TUSAS 591)
    Includes bibliographical references and index.
    ISBN 0-8057-7639-7 (alk. paper)
    1. Godwin, Gail—Criticism and interpretation. I. Title.
II. Series.
PS3557.0315Z68   1992
813'.54—dc20
                                                    91-27001
                                                    CIP

for Nina Baym

Contents

Preface

I first heard Gail Godwin's voice on the "Today" show in the fall of 1987. Her seventh novel, *A Southern Family*, had just been published. I was already deep into this book. It was unlikely that a seven-minute interview would provide insights that would alter my thinking, but I had just finished reading *A Southern Family* for the first time and was interested in what Jane Pauley would ask, as well as in what Godwin would say.

Eventually, my chapter on that novel would become the conclusion for this book; eventually, I would meet Gail Godwin. But perhaps none of that would have happened as it did if I had not heard her voice that early morning in 1987. For when Godwin spoke, much to my surprise, she had a southern accent. Of course, I knew that she had grown up in the South, but I also knew that it had been many years since she had lived there, that she had lived in Europe, the Midwest, Manhattan, and rural New York, among other exotic locales. Surely, I thought, she would not sound like people in the western North Carolina mountains anymore.

But she did. A native of western South Carolina, I sound pretty much the same way. Thus, we had a bond; because of that bond, I was not intimidated when we met. And meeting her confirmed for me that my instincts about her work were sound.

My sense that I could do justice to Godwin and her work because she spoke with the familiar accent of our region is, of course, a flimsy peg on which to hang one's critical hat. But on just such fragilities, minute turns of mind and confidence, does the world revolve in Gail Godwin's fiction. Perhaps that is one reason I have felt at home in the world of her novels and stories. It is a place where someone might be hesitant to speak before she can gauge the reception she will receive, a place where a woman can't help constructing the circumstances of her actions with the subtlest attention to detail and nuance.

I first read Gail Godwin on a visit to my mother—in *Redbook*, which published a condensation of *A Mother and Two Daughters*. I next read *The Odd Woman* when a friend thought I might be interested because one of the characters, Sonia Marks, reminded my friend of a professor I had studied with at the University of Illinois. So I bought a paperback of *The Odd Woman*, intending to read only the parts that might be about the person I knew.

I read the entire novel. What got me was the difference in the depth and texture of this novel and the condensation of another I'd read in *Redbook*. That had been good, but this was something else altogether. This was important writing.

To have found my way to Godwin through this maze of coincidence is, finally, a wonderful Godwinesque story, influenced by a mother figure, connected, however loosely, to my own life at Illinois, nudged along by a female friend, following a path from limited knowledge, skepticism, and doubt to rich appreciation and respect, topped off with expectation of more and better things to come.

Gail Godwin lives in Woodstock, New York, in a striking cedar home perched atop what might be called a "little" mountain (although probably not by someone who grew up with the wonders of the Blue Ridge). When I visited her there in November 1988, it came as no surprise that she was, with everything else, a good hostess. The wonder of the visit was the depth and complexity that lay beneath the smoothly polished, just-right surface of the place and the event. After an early morning walk down the little mountain to have a look at the construction of the Green Chapel (the guest house Godwin and her companion, Robert Starer, were building, partly as a place to provide writers, musicians, and other artists with a quiet, productive space for creating), we went up the stairs to Godwin's study, the place where she writes.

There we spent the morning talking about her books and other people's, about writing itself. She told me a wonderful story about a visitor who preceded me the Friday before my Sunday arrival. The young woman, who attended a nearby college, was quite taken by Ursula DeVane, the mentor to young Justin Stokes in *The Finishing School*. Clearly, she thought, Godwin could play Ursula to her Justin, and the young woman, having made her pilgrimage by Greyhound bus, found herself disappointed that the real woman she met did not suit her needs. The real Gail Godwin was a bit too much like the grown-up Justin, not nearly enough like Ursula DeVane. As a reader, I much preferred the grown-up Justin to Ursula, and talking about the differences in Justin and Ursula led us to a discussion of narrative technique, which led us to much more.

By the time Godwin drove me back to the Albany airport, we were trying to figure out why a mother might leave her six-year-old daughter—the genesis of *Father's Melancholy Daughter,* the novel Godwin was working on at the time. The daughter, her main character, was something of a mystery as well, and I was the mother of a thoroughly modern girl. So we talked on and on, trying to figure it all out, or as much of it as would fit in the two-hour drive. We were deep into what fiction is, how it works, where it can take us.

Although the South plays a significant role in Godwin's novels beginning with *Glass People,* many critics and readers have not emphasized the region's role in her work. Nor did her name often appear in listings of contemporary southern writers before her seventh novel's title forced the association. Prior to the publication of *A Southern Family,* Godwin was perhaps most often pigeonholed as a "woman" writer, meaning not only that she was a woman but that her work was written for and would appeal to a predominantly female audience.

There is much in Godwin's eight novels and two collections of stories to discuss with these issues—her region and her gender— in mind. But, like her alter ego in *A Southern Family,* Clare Campion, Gail Godwin surely wants and deserves to break a potentially deadly twin embrace. For Clare Campion the deadly twins are region and family; for Godwin, region and gender. But the crux of the matter is the same: both women, both writers, they want to be free of externally imposed limitations.

Godwin has staked out for herself an increasingly tricky literary ground. More than many writers of her generation, she writes out of a self-conscious awareness of the tradition of the novel in English. References—direct and indirect—to her literary ancestors abound in her novels and stories. Readers who fail to recognize Godwin's allusions to D. H. Lawrence, Henry James, George Eliot, and a dozen other named or unnamed authors or works will miss some of the richness and intelligence of her writings. But at the same time she is experimenting, writing about characters who test the forms and conventions of their lives, and exploring the dark inner recesses and the mystical and spiritual strivings of her characters.

In this study I have attempted to free Godwin's novels from the themes, concerns, and techniques most often associated with "southern" writing and "women's" writing, without denying or foolishly deemphasizing those obvious threads. But other threads merit equally serious attention.

In chapter 1 I seek to establish the strong autobiographical elements in Godwin's novels at the same time I define the ironic twist that those elements inevitably receive in the transforming process of art. The layers of expectation and convention in life and art that are the targets of and the motivation for Godwin's ironic posture are not entirely separate from region and gender. Southern women are mythic for their ability to twist and shape, shadow and highlight reality in much the way a talented artist does. But

Godwin's art transcends those native talents to connect with larger traditions of the novel in America and Europe.

Then, in chapter 2, which deals with *The Perfectionists* and *Glass People,* the first two novels, I define the fictional idiom of Godwin's work: a youthful, intelligent, ambitious yet doubting heroine in search of her best life; a series of models she uses to test herself against; and a provocative interplay between the plot and its characters and the telling itself, the narrative strategy of the novels.

Chapter 3 focuses on *The Odd Woman* and *Violet Clay,* arguing that the idiom defined in the earlier novels benefits from increased narrative sophistication and control and from an expanded sense of the heroine—the "typical" Godwin woman—to include a rich relationship with meaningful work. Chapter 4, which deals with *A Mother and Two Daughters* and *The Finishing School,* continues to examine the expanding idiom. Here, the telling points are multiple protagonists and more ambitious, ambiguous points of view.

Finally, in *A Southern Family,* the subject of chapter 5, Godwin is able to confront her region head on. But, with typical irony, *A Southern Family* is really more noteworthy for its continuing expansion of narrative sophistication, for its paradigmatic interweaving of life and art, and for the self-reflexive relationship between Godwin's form and content.

I have tried to let the characters in Godwin's novels live truly, have tried to discuss them and their stories in the context of what the author seems to have set out to do and in light of the directions the characters themselves took her on the way to the finished stories and novels. I have focused on character and plot because Godwin is a writer who demands of herself characters who ring true, who fill up the page with their breathing, substantial selves, and who pursue specific goals and confront specific obstacles.

I have also analyzed how Godwin puts her novels together—who narrates them and how those narrators structure their tales. For almost any southerner can tell a story. It is in the shaping, the loving and thoughtful selection and structuring, that art happens. And it is Godwin's artistry that this book seeks to examine and celebrate.

Chronology

1937   Gail Kathleen Godwin born 18 June, Birmingham, Alabama, daughter of Mose Winston Godwin and Kathleen Krahenbuhl Godwin.

1939   Kathleen and Gail move to Durham, North Carolina, to live with Thomas and Edna Krahenbuhl; Thomas Krahenbuhl dies.

1940   Kathleen, Gail, and Edna Krahenbuhl move to Weaverville, North Carolina.

1948   Kathleen Godwin marries Frank Cole.

1955–1957   Attends Peace Junior College, Raleigh, North Carolina.

1958   Mose Godwin commits suicide.

1959   B.A. in journalism from the University of North Carolina at Chapel Hill.

1959–1960   Reporter for *Miami Herald*.

1960   Marries Douglas Kennedy, a *Herald* photographer.

1961   Divorces Kennedy.

1961–1965   Works in U.S. Travel Service at American Embassy, London.

1965   Marries Ian Marshall, a British physician and psychotherapist.

1966   Divorces Marshall; returns to U.S. and works as editorial assistant at *Saturday Evening Post*.

1968   M.A. in English, University of Iowa.

1970   *The Perfectionists*.

1971   Ph.D. in English, University of Iowa.

1971–1972   Fellow of Center for Advanced Study, University of Illinois at Champaign–Urbana.

1972–1973   Lecturer, University of Iowa Writers' Workshop.

1972   *Glass People*; Edna Krahenbuhl dies.

1974–1975   National Endowment for the Arts grant.

1974   *The Odd Woman*; National Book Award nomination.

1975–1976   Guggenheim fellowship.

1975   Libretto for *The Last Lover* (composer, Robert Starer).

1976   *Dream Children*; American specialist, United States Information Service in Brazil.

1977   Lecturer at Vassar College.

1978   *Violet Clay*; lecturer at Columbia University; National Book Award nomination.

1979   Libretto for *Apollonia* (composer, Robert Starer).

1981   Recipient, award in literature, American Academy and Institute of Arts and Letters; libretto for *Anna Margarita's Will* (composer, Robert Starer); lecturer at Columbia University.

1982   *A Mother and Two Daughters*; National Book Award nomination.

1983   *Mr. Bedford and the Muses*; death of half-brother Tommy Cole.

1984   *The Finishing School.*

1985   Edits *Best American Short Stories.*

1986   Chief fiction judge for National Book Awards.

1987   *A Southern Family.*

1988   Named distinguished alumna, the University of North Carolina; Thomas Wolfe Award for *A Southern Family.*

1989   Janet Kafka Prize for *A Southern Family*; founding of St. Hilda's Press; libretto for *Remembering Felix* (composer, Robert Starer); Kathleen Krahenbuhl Godwin Cole dies in car accident.

1991   *Father Melancholy's Daughter.*

Chapter One
Peeling Away the Mask and Masques of Fiction

Readers familiar with Gail Godwin's fiction, whether they realize it or not, are also to some degree familiar with her life, and anyone curious about the author's life would find her novels and stories as informative as other available sources. In "The Uses of Autobiography," Godwin argues that for any writer, no matter how a protagonist is disguised, that character is in some way a reflection of the author's self or at least some aspect of that self. Of her own work specifically she says, "All my protagonists—slapstick, allegorical, disguised by gender or species, occupation or social class, or hardly disguised at all—are parts of myself."[1] She cites an idea expressed by Dickens biographer Edgar Johnson as the reason behind this necessary, inevitable link between autobiography and fiction: experience not profoundly realized within cannot be vividly or profoundly rendered without.

The uninitiated reader or scholar attempting to get a quick handle on Godwin as a writer must resist the temptation to indulge in the easy biographical criticism that such sentiments as these, voiced by the author herself, invite. For Gail Godwin the woman and Gail Godwin the author are too complex, their wits and wiles too sharp, to provide such a simple handle on the woman or her work. Godwin's title for an essay about her mother, "My Mother, the Writer: Master of a Thousand Disguises," characterizes her, a woman who also once earned her living as a writer, as a master of disguise. In this essay, Godwin deals with the complex relationship between the masks the writer uses to transform the raw material of autobiography into the art of fiction and the masks used to negotiate the treacherous territory of daily life in a way that both produces that material and provides the space and freedom for the necessary transformation.

Godwin's fiction is firmly grounded in her own experience; the direct correlations between life and art are perhaps more obvious and more numerous than with many other writers. She is also her mother's daughter in that she too is a master of disguise, of the beguiling and often dangerous deceptions southern belles have been famous for at least since Scarlett O'Hara first batted her eyelashes at a naive and unsuspecting Charles Hamilton.

Readers just entering the rich world of Godwin's fiction would do well to
keep the image of Mr. Hamilton before them as a warning about the fate
likely to befall the gullible once they fall into the hands of a master deceiver,
a supreme fictionist. Mr. Hamilton was dead of measles before he could
catch his breath; Scarlett will weave her magic for as long as there are books
or movies.

A Small, Manless Family

Gail Godwin was born in Birmingham, Alabama, on 18 June 1937, to
Mose Winston and Kathleen Krahenbuhl Godwin, who met when
Kathleen's dog bit a limping Mose. When Godwin was two, her parents separated. Godwin and her mother moved first to Durham, then Weaverville,
North Carolina, and finally to Asheville, North Carolina, where Godwin
grew up. Asheville provides the setting for at least portions of four of
Godwin's novels—*Glass People, The Odd Woman, A Mother and Two Daughters,* and *A Southern Family;* the city also appears in several short stories. Its
prominence in her work makes her the clear literary heir of the city's other
great chronicler, Thomas Wolfe.

After her parents' separation Godwin and her mother lived with her maternal grandparents until Thomas Krahenbuhl's death in 1939. By the time
she was five, Godwin was settled into life with her mother and her maternal
grandmother, who kept house for the small, unconventional family while
Kathleen Godwin became the breadwinner. Mose Godwin was, by all ac-
counts, a handsome, charming man, full of dreams and expectations, but
his ability to bring those hopes to fruition appears to have been limited. He
taught tennis in Florida and took people on bicycle tours. The character of
Ambrose Clay in Godwin's fourth novel, *Violet Clay,* has been cited as a
portrait of the author's father. From the time she had her tonsils removed at
seven until a beach trip she took with him and her stepmother in 1955,
Godwin did not see her father. In an excerpt from her journals dated 30
May 1982, Godwin remembers that trip and tries to imagine how her father must have felt about her.

The period of this journal entry coincides with the time in which Godwin
would have been working on *Mr. Bedford and the Muses* and *The Finishing
School,* books primarily concerned with how perspective is altered by time,
how memory adjusts, corrects, forgives much that the younger self cannot.
Having finished *Violet Clay,* with its transformed version of her father, and
having begun work on books concerned with the revisionist quality of
memory, Godwin made this entry: "[My father] must have found me

scarifying: both in the sense of my being selfish like him, and in the sense that I was not the malleable, appreciative daughter I am sure he thought he had the right to expect."[2] It was written while she vacationed at Pawley's Island, South Carolina, a retreat not far north of Charleston, the ancestral home of her fictional Clay family, and the setting of the dramatic denouement of *A Southern Family*. The sentiments are a real-life counterpart to the thinking of the narrators and heroines in the stories and the novel that were her fictional concerns at that time.

This complex interweaving of life and art and the often overlapping subject matter and locales for Godwin's fiction also demonstrates the inherent irony in hindsight or memory-revised vision. In 1955 Godwin was reunited with her handsome, selfish father, who was at least pleased with her appearance, if not manner, but, as the author writes from the perspective of 1982, the tensions and disappointments she sensed beneath the surface of their visit would, in three years, overtake and consume her father. Mose Godwin committed suicide (as does his fictional counterpart, Ambrose Clay) in 1958, during Godwin's junior year at the University of North Carolina.

Psychologists specializing in the study of the family, particularly families touched by divorce, would probably argue that the absence of a parent can and often does exert as great an influence on a child as the presence of the other parent. In her introduction to the *Best American Short Stories 1985*, which she edited, Godwin admits to a special weakness for stories about fathers.[3] Certainly, *Violet Clay* and, to a lesser extent, *Glass People, The Odd Woman, A Mother and Two Daughters,* and *The Finishing School* resonate with the feeling of loss associated with the absence of a father figure, and, with the exception of Leonard Strickland in *A Mother and Two Daughters,* the father figure bears considerable resemblance to Mose Godwin.

But Godwin's fiction argues even more convincingly for the inescapable influence of her mother on her work. *Glass People, The Odd Woman, The Finishing School, A Mother and Two Daughters,* and *A Southern Family* all have at their core the importance of the mother-daughter relationship. No matter what other concerns these novels raise, that central connection is crucial to the understanding and growth of Godwin's protagonists. In an essay entitled "Becoming a Writer," Godwin recalls the two female role models that offered themselves to her in her childhood—her grandmother who cooked and her mother who wrote. At five, Godwin says, she chose the typewriter over the stove.[4]

Kathleen Godwin, a graduate of Furman University and the University of North Carolina, with an M.A. in English and drama, was a reporter for the *Asheville Citizen-Times*. She supplemented the family income by writ-

ing romance fiction for pulp magazines and by teaching classes at the local
college (now the University of North Carolina at Asheville) to servicemen
returning from World War II and taking advantage of the GI Bill to edu-
cate themselves into a position to take jobs away from the women, such as
Kathleen Godwin, who had held them while the men were away at war. In
one of these classes, a course in Romantic literature, Kathleen Godwin met
Frank Cole, whom she married in 1948. Cole is the source of several of
Godwin's stepfather characters (Ray in *The Odd Woman* and Ralph in *A
Southern Family*, most significantly).

Much of Kathleen Godwin's work was published under the pseudonym
Charlotte Ashe, which, according to Godwin in "My Mother, the Writer,"
was an identity that allowed a voice for the hidden, suppressed self within
her mother, the part of her that she had to hush in order to continue being
Kathleen Cole. Her mother's specialty as a writer was the representative heroine, the stuff of the stock fiction typical of the genre that earned her the
income she needed, the antithesis of the singular heroine, the "passing
strange" character that most interests her daughter ("Becoming," 236).

By cleverly subverting the romance genre at the same time that she ex-
ploited it, Kathleen Godwin/Charlotte Ashe managed, as Godwin notes in
"My Mother, the Writer," to get away with much that would have surprised,
if not horrified, the editors of *Love Short Stories*, the pulp magazine that
published many of her stories. Godwin/Ashe was literally a master of disguise at work. But her success in the romance market did, finally, produce
or foster limitations that prevented Kathleen Cole from expanding her career as a writer. When she had her agent submit a novel, the publisher wrote
back that she "writes like an angel at times. At other times, she is much too
facile . . . and sentimental."[5]

Eventually, as Godwin chronicles in *The Odd Woman* and *A Southern
Family*, Kathleen Cole gave up on herself as writer and buried Charlotte
Ashe forever behind the mask of wifehood. Frank Cole became successful as
a builder; the necessity that drove the writing career diminished and finally
disappeared; the woman who had used her deceptive abilities to go beyond
the limits of her pulp genre began to turn those same abilities toward the
necessity of being a proper southern wife and mother and social creature.
This strange, aborted career of Kathleen Cole, with its layers of masks and
masques, as Godwin calls them in "My Mother, the Writer," suggests an almost Yeatsian quality of trying to separate the dancer from the dance, as the
grown daughter, successful novelist herself, tries to find the essence of her
mother.

Godwin says, "Charlotte Ashe, quite a bit of her, found her way into Gail

Godwin. I have learned to recognize her—and to salute her (warily!), that discontented trickstress of multiple disguises, whenever, after thinking I have been writing about one thing, I discover behind it her covert designs" ("Mother," 51). She goes on to say that after finishing *A Southern Family,* one of her most overtly autobiographical books, she found herself drawn to a "completely made-up" novel that allows a mother to run off with another woman. She posits the possibility that this totally fictional plot may, in fact, under the layers of disguise and the masques of fiction, be just another of her attempts at "getting something important back together: two warring sides of the same woman" ("Mother," 51), a woman whose conflicting selves have their origins in the struggle between Kathleen Cole and Charlotte Ashe.

The decision to take on a "completely made-up" story, only to discover that its origins perhaps lie in her mother's decades-long struggle between two aspects of herself indicates that Godwin, as a novelist, has always faced the question of where autobiography and art meet and separate. Her first stab at a novel ended with a 1959 rejection of her attempt to rewrite one of her mother's rejected novels, *The Otherwise Virgins,* a title whose ironies include the dark twist of mind implicit in the Charlotte Ashe aspect of her mother's persona. That this first effort was rejected seems less important than the fact that it was intimately connected to the mother and her career—the stuff of Godwin's real life, with all its ironies and complexities.

In "Becoming a Writer" Godwin faces this question of art and life, fact and fiction: "Fact and fiction: fiction and fact. Which stops where, and how much to put in of each? At what point does regurgitated autobiography graduate into memory shaped by art? How do you know when to stop telling it as it is, and make it into what it ought to be—or what would make a better story?" ("Becoming," 236).

If this set of questions is, a decade later, used to evaluate Godwin's own career, it is perhaps important also to consider her assessment of problems in her unpublished early work, given in answer to these questions in 1980. At that time she felt that these early efforts suffered in very specific ways: "Either they had the ring of self-consciousness about them, or else they started too slowly and petered out before I ever got to the interesting material that had inspired me in the first place, or else they were so close to the current problems of my own life that I couldn't gain the proper distance and perspective" ("Becoming," 246).

Of the five books written before this statement, the last published was *Violet Clay,* the novel that features Godwin's fullest fictional treatment of her father. In it her protagonist, a painter, finds the perspective to take her beyond the stock romance-novel illustrations she has been cranking out to sustain her drinking and her love life. All the while she has been deceiving herself that the work she's selling her soul for is only temporary, a stop-gap measure that will be unnecessary once she gets her life on track and finds the time and emotional energy to pursue higher art. Violet Clay, Godwin's alter ego here, turns the corner and heads toward her true art through the story of another woman. In a similar way, the novel that follows *Violet Clay* and Godwin's assessment of the problems in her earlier work is *A Mother and Two Daughters,* a novel modeled not after Godwin's own life but loosely along lines suggested by that of her oldest friend, Pat Verhulst, to whom the novel is dedicated.[6]

Thus, *A Mother and Two Daughters* appears to mark a turning point in Godwin's career. The novelist moves away from material so directly linked to her own life and finds a position in relation to her new material that allows her to extend the boundaries of the territory that had previously comprised her fictional world. Coincidentally, this novel brought Godwin her first extraordinary commercial success, her third National Book Award nomination, and a broad name recognition that she shares with only a handful of writers of her generation.

The Impulse to Write

After high school Godwin attended Peace Junior College in Raleigh, North Carolina, from 1955 through 1957, then went on to the University of North Carolina at Chapel Hill (the alma mater of Thomas Wolfe, Kathleen Krahenbuhl, and Mose Godwin), where she received her bachelor's degree in journalism in 1959. From Chapel Hill, she went to the *Miami Herald* as a reporter. Within a year, her rewrite of *Otherwise Virgins* had been rejected, and she had "embellished stories"[7] and been fired with some reluctance from the *Herald* by her editor, who lamented his failure to make a good reporter of promising material. She had also married *Herald* photographer Douglas Kennedy. The marriage lasted less than a year. Her return to Asheville and her mother, transported by her stepfather, is a scene portrayed in several places in Godwin's fiction. Godwin next went to London and worked for the U.S. Travel Service at the American Embassy from 1961 until 1965. Those years provide the background for Godwin's novella, "Mr. Bedford," and her meeting and eventually marrying British psychotherapist Ian Marshall is the stuff out of which her first novel, *The Perfectionists,* was generated.

Godwin met Marshall when they were both students in a fiction class at the City Literary Institute in London. They married only two months later.

In "Becoming a Writer" Godwin, quoting D. H. Lawrence, describes the relationship as a "nervous attachment rather than a sexual love" ("Becoming," 250). That marriage, too, lasted only about a year, but Godwin credits Marshall with making it possible for her to become the writer she knew she could be. In "Becoming a Writer" she acknowledges that his Scientology-inspired questioning technique forced her to recognize her fear of failure. (The influence of Scientology in Godwin's life becomes a subject for humor in "Some Side Effects of Time Travel," collected in *Dream Children*.)

While Godwin was a student at Peace College, a Scottish Presbyterian minister conducted a retreat there. For the same class that generated the marriage to Marshall, she wrote a story based on the minister's visit. Orginally titled "The Illumined Moment—and Consequences" and later retitled "An Intermediate Stop" and collected in *Dream Children,* that story proved the solution to Godwin's future once her marriage to Marshall ended. It got her admitted to the Writers' Workshop at Iowa and became the first of her stories accepted for publication (by the *North American Review*).

Godwin's impulse to write long precedes her matriculation at Iowa, however. She began keeping a journal at 13, a habit that persists even now. She says, "I made my first diary, with half-sheets of notebook paper, cardboard, and yarn, and I wrote in it passionately, because I felt there was nobody else like me and I had to know why—or why not."[8] Through her juvenile fiction, Godwin gradually discovered that the process of writing allows one to take control, to shape oneself and one's experience toward a goal, in much the way that a writer shapes a protagonist in fiction. This concept of life mirroring fiction, Godwin argues, allows an individual access to the heroic.[9]

In her juvenilia, Godwin has observed a pattern of thematic concerns that persists in her adult work: the individual's struggle to coexist with authorities and to make peace with the social structure while still retaining individuality; the role of choices and decision making in life; the essential question for artists: will you have the price of admission at art's gate?; and the consequences of aspiration and thwarted aspiration ("Uses," 7–8). Each of these childhood concerns finds its way into almost every story and novel Godwin has written as a adult.

Thus, when she arrived in Iowa City in 1967, twice divorced, having worked as a journalist and a government employee, and having found her first "good angel" of writing ("Becoming," 247) in her teacher at London's City Literary Institute, she brought with her three decades of formative experience as well. At Iowa one of Godwin's teachers was Kurt Vonnegut, and John Irving was a classmate (Vespa, 69). The Iowa landscape finds its way into *A Mother and Two Daughters* and *A Southern Family,* but Godwin left the country's premier writing program with more than famous friends and memories of the landscape. *The Perfectionists,* her first novel, was published while she was still a student there, and from the time she received her doctorate in English in 1971 she has earned her living as a writer, with only intermittent teaching and research appointments at places such as the Center for Advanced Study at the University of Illinois at Champaign–Urbana (which provides the setting for portions of *The Odd Woman*), Iowa, Vassar, and Columbia.

After four years, winter and summer, of graduate school at Iowa, Godwin spent two months in the summer of 1972 at the artists' colony at Yaddo. Her goal for her residence was to complete the historical sections, the Cleva story, of the novel that would become *The Odd Woman.* In writing about that summer almost 15 years later, Godwin recalls that the setting of Yaddo itself captured history and held as much promise and threat for her as it would have for the fictional sisters of the earlier era about which she was writing.[10]

Assigned to the room that once belonged to Katrina Trask, the colony's founder, Godwin says, "As soon as I unpacked I began writing. It would have seemed ungrateful not to" ("Yaddo," 3). What she wrote, at first, was roughly 100 pages of a story she then called *The Villain.* This work was never published but was stored and labeled "Abandoned early section of *The Odd Woman*" ("Yaddo," 3). After these pages were scrapped, Godwin experienced what she calls a "reassuring haunting" that led her to a new vision, renewed energies, and a fully formed and essentially final first chapter for *The Odd Woman.* The image of the "haunting" deals with the quality of light, an image that in the novel refers to the protagonist's sensing the presence of her recently deceased grandmother. (The supernatural quality of this experience also suggests the recurring element of nonrational experience in the stories in *Dream Children.*)

This emotional turning point translated into fictional technique for Godwin by altering her concept of narrative structure. She learned to see narration as "a kind of shimmering circle rather than the old straight-line point-to-point" ("Yaddo," 3). The result, the final form of *The Odd Woman,* indicates that her time at Yaddo and the transformation in her thinking that it produced were, in fact, a crucial link in Godwin's move from promising young novice to accomplished professional. The texture and complexity of *The Odd Woman* go far beyond what she achieved in the two earlier novels, and the narrative and structural variation that enhances all of Godwin's subsequent work can be traced to the recognition that her favorite story, that of an independent young woman trying to live her best life, need not, in fact, perhaps had best not, be told in a linear fashion.

At Yaddo she also met Robert Starer, the composer, with whom she has collaborated on several operas, writing the librettos to accompany his music. *The Odd Woman* and *Violet Clay* are both dedicated to Starer, who has been Godwin's companion for almost two decades.

An Idiom of One's Own

Although *The Odd Woman* marks a significant leap forward in Godwin's career, from the beginning she has been considered a serious and accomplished fiction writer. Joyce Carol Oates called *The Perfectionists* "engrossing and mysterious,"[11] and Robert Scholes pronounced it "an excellent piece of work, shrewdly observed and carefully crafted," going on to note that it possessed an "eerie tension" and seemed to be "a combination of Jane Austen and D. H. Lawrence" and concluding that the book "is an extraordinary accomplishment."[12] He does, however, with some apologies for the politically sensitive nature of such comments, call it "very much a woman's novel" (Scholes, 37) and announces that his comments are to be made in that context. Resisting the urge to patronize such good and clever work by considering it as a first novel, his "principal criticism" has to do with its "resolute femininity" (Scholes, 38).

Such damning with lavish, gender-specific praise has limited Godwin and many of her contemporaries throughout their careers. It is the literary equivalent of how female athletes, on junior-high playing fields and in Olympic stadiums, are subjected to comments such as, "Well, that's good—for a girl." Godwin's own assessment of her early unpublished work as self-conscious or slow or petering out before the truly interesting material is reached or too close to her own life ("Becoming," 246) provides more insight into *The Perfectionists* than reviewers' more generous praise. The lavishness of even such qualified acknowledgment of excellence does, however, indicate the enthusiasm with which Godwin's work has been greeted from the beginning.

Much more interesting is the early recognition of Godwin's affinities with Austen and Lawrence, an unlikely literary couple. *The Perfectionists* begins Godwin's very Austen-like exploration of the manners governing the lives of a generation of women born during a complex era of change for females. The later novels make the similarities to Austen's novels of manners even more significant by defining Godwin's typical protagonist as a specifically southern woman, thereby making the manners and mores of that region integral to the fiction. Godwin also shares Austen's quiet irony and wit, which help to enlarge the significance of the experiences of a relatively thin slice of society.

When a healthy dose of Laurentian sexuality and quirky subterranean psychological insight is added to the careful portrait of a generation's manners, as it is in *The Perfectionists* and, in varying portions, in most of Godwin's work, the charted territory of women's fiction begins to feel inadequate. It is as if the author of *The Perfectionists* has consciously decided to strike out for the unmapped regions where manners and deeper, darker psychological truths collide—and, clearly, provide fertile ground for sowing fiction. Godwin has said that she wants to write about the realm of reality still suppressed by the current market (echoes of Charlotte Ashe and Kathleen Cole's dilemma, of course), even in "liberated" times—"the dark blossomings, the suppressed (or veiled) truths" ("Becoming," 234).

Thus, being female and southern and inevitably influenced by the manners governing that life, but also living in a post-Laurentian era of personal and sexual freedom, Godwin discovers, in her first novel, the oxymoronic quality of an existence governed by these particular truths that will be the genesis of her personal fictional idiom.

Anatole Broyard, who was less fond of some of Godwin's later work, called *Glass People* the expression of a "contemporary woman's 'new consciousness' " in a "good novel."[13] Since the early 1970s Godwin and dozens of women novelists have tried to define the new consciousness of their time, but the novels of this era that have a chance to survive and to transcend the limitations of that goal fit the second half of Broyard's description: they are good novels. This book aims to demonstrate that, in Godwin's case, this judgment of excellence is not a subjective appreciation but one based on careful study of Godwin's craftsmanship. The most overlooked strength of her work is her ability to write a carefully crafted novel, with a sound plot and clearly defined characters, an interesting and appropriate narrative technique, a control and mastery of form.

Godwin's reputation rests primarily on her novels, so much so that she has sometimes been introduced as the author of nine novels rather than seven novels and two collections of stories. Both *Dream Children* and *Mr. Bedford and the Muses* were well received, and both provide significant insights into Godwin's development as a writer, her theories of fiction, and the novels that overshadow them.

Both collections are full of references, characters, settings, and scenes that recall one or more of the novels. The main character in many of the stories is the typical Godwin woman and appears as a writer much more frequently than in the novels, where Clare Campion of *A Southern Family* is the first writer-heroine Godwin creates. In fact, all but one of the stories in the second collection deal specifically with the development of a writer who is the main character, and seven of the 15 stories in *Dream Children* also feature writers as main characters.

One function of this focus in the short fiction is to provide a fictional anatomy that details the author's sense of the writer's life. Coupled with the instances in which the short stories reflect and echo the novels, these collections can be read as footnotes to Godwin's more significant work, but that would be unfair to the integrity of the individual stories: they are full of their own insights, freshness of perspective, surprises and moments of recognition and are significant collections as a whole. Much more than is the case with many contemporary story collections, Godwin's two books of short stories have a unity of theme and crafted structure as collections that carry them beyond mere addenda to her longer fiction.

In many ways the two collections represent different but equally important facets of Godwin's sensibilities and tendencies as a writer. *Dream Children,* whose stories began appearing in magazines in 1971, is the younger writer's book, and its controlling theme is the testing and exploration of limits. Its characters are people who have gone beyond limits of some kind; its resolutions often occur beyond the boundaries of physical reality. *Mr. Bedford and the Muses,* on the other hand, contains stories that first appeared in magazines beginning in 1976, the year of *Dream Children's* publication, and the novella and five short stories that make up the later collection are about learning to live within limits, about characters who come to accept security and accomplishment or who come to accommodate lesser lives with a modicum of grace and dignity.

Once a reader comes to terms with the individual stories and grasps the unity and coherence of the collections, this dichotomy in the themes and characters of the two books serves as either a good introduction to the conflicts and paradoxes that dominate all of Godwin's characters or a helpful summation of what is already familiar from a knowledge of the novels. The richness and depth in Godwin's short fiction indicate that it deserves its own study, apart from this book, which concentrates on the novels.

Godwin's reputation was firmly established with *A Mother and Two Daughters,* her fifth novel. After its popular success, a new set of expectations (and reservations)—those of the "popular" novelist—found its way into the responses to her work. The result of such a curious mix of criteria and expectations is inevitably an increased possibility of conscious or unconscious misreading. A work is sometimes judged according to the pigeonhole the reviewer wants to make Godwin's literary home—feminist novelist, woman's

writer, mystical writer—and any other context of the work is ignored. Sometimes Godwin is presumed to have had a particular sort of novel in mind but
to have confused that sort with several other things, thus sending mixed signals about the direction she is trying to go. Rarely are novels reviewed,
Godwin's or anyone's, in the context of the author's career as a whole, but
that is how the most interesting and significant observations about Godwin's
work can be made.

A good example of the way a reviewer can miss part of what Godwin is
doing in a novel by ignoring narrative technique is Gene Lyons's review of
The Finishing School. He says that "Whatever Godwin's virtues as a novelist, she has no sense of humor."[14] He goes on to cite examples, mentioning
the plastic runners that protect the carpet in the home of Mona Mott, the
aunt of the protagonist and narrator, Justin Stokes. Justin, at 13, is horrified
by the runners and sees them as a reflection of everything that is wrong with
her aunt and her way of life. If there were no irony involved, then Godwin
would indeed seem humorless. What Lyons misses in *The Finishing School*
is a narrative strategy (to be discussed in chapter 4) new to Godwin.

Godwin's broadest and most universal praise from reviewers has come for
the two novels that have been her greatest commercial successes as well. That
fact again raises questions about the power of reviews in a media-dominated
society. Does an appearance on *Today* sell books? Does a comment in the *New
York Times* that a book is an author's best automatically increase sales? This
sort of speculation is as applicable to other authors as it is to Godwin, and
commercial success does not mean that a book lacks literary merit. Just as understanding Godwin's narrative technique can reveal the humor in *The Finishing School*, an awareness of how *A Mother and Two Daughters* differs from
her previous work can help explain its popular success.

A Southern Family uses another narrative approach entirely new for
Godwin—multiple limited points of view. To the reader who has watched
her development as novelist from *The Perfectionists* through *The Finishing
School*, this new technique embodies the strengths of much of her previous
work at the same time it marks a breakthrough in the effort to broaden
scope and to balance the author's deep awareness of the dark side of human
experience with a vision that embodies more faith and hope.

Her Own Best Critic and Literary Diplomat

Godwin has been, in many ways, her own best critic. This is an odd position for an artist, but none of her reviewers or scholarly critics has shown the
insight into her strengths and weaknesses that Godwin herself has. After a

decade as a published novelist, she analyzed those strengths and weaknesses in "Becoming a Writer":

> I think the most serious danger to my writing is my predilection for shapeliness. How I love "that nice circular Greek shape" my mother spoke of; or a nice, neat conclusion, with all the edges tucked under. And this sometimes leads me to "wrap up" things, to force dramatic revelations at the expense of allowing the truth to reveal itself in slow, shy, and often problematical glimpses.
>
> But my serious danger is also my strength. And so I must fight its temptations and preserve its rights at the same time. For it is the part of my talent that *selects* from what Henry James called "the rattle and the rumble" of ordinary existence, and fashions these literal happenings into another kind of truth called a story. ("Becoming," 253)

Before her first book was published, even before she went to Iowa, Godwin realized that the best source for true fiction lay outside the easy, the pat, the too predictable. In a journal entry for 1 January 1966, written while she was living in London, Godwin says, "This is important: this is near to something: for me to be 'straightforward' would be the biggest lie of all. My way is weaving cunningly through mazes; not chopping down the mazes with a razor-straight, unyielding disposition."[15]

She goes on in this same entry to explore the difference in other people's truth and what she wanted to find as truth in her writing. She says, "What little knowledge we have, really. It would be so easy to cotton onto Hubbard [the founder of Scientology] or Jung or Ian [her second husband] and say: 'Yes, life can be explained by eight dynamics or seven levels or six archetypes.' *All this is true,* yet there is always more, always an extra piece that doesn't fit in the category" ("Keeping," 78).

Although some critics and reviewers have found the world of Godwin's fiction too narrow and personal, too introverted for their taste, few contemporary authors are as willing as she has been to examine in print her methods, her sources, and her growth as a writer. In fact, one of the most interesting and little noted aspects of Godwin's career is her role as a citizen of the literary community. When she wrote the introduction for the eighth annual Pushcart Prize anthology in 1983, she used the occasion to celebrate the importance of little magazines and small presses to the general well-being of American letters, and even after becoming a best-selling novelist Godwin has continued to contribute to literary journals. In 1989 she made her commitment to such noncommercial outlets more tangible by founding St. Hilda's Press, in conjunction with the Episcopal diocese of Western

North Carolina. Named for Saint Hilda (A.D. 614–674), the founding abbess of a monastery with communities for both men and women and a woman known for her passion for learning, the press publishes books, tracts, and music of artistic and spiritual value that might not find an outlet in the world of commercial publishing. St. Hilda's Press intends, in Godwin's words, "to revive old treasures and encourage new flowerings and, thus, in the spirit of our namesake, minister to the complex needs of our own time."[16]

In 1986 Godwin served as chief judge for the National Book Award's fiction prize, overseeing a controversial selection process that ended with one nominee, Peter Taylor, withdrawing his name from consideration just before the award was made to E. L. Doctorow, who commented that literature was "not a horse race." After the decision was made, Godwin said that the committee of judges had taken "three winners and created a winner and two losers."[17] Such a public forum for complex private decision making reveals considerable behind-the-scenes turmoil, but Godwin maintained her commitment to active involvement.

When such public activity is combined with essays and articles on the writing process and reviews of novels by contemporaries that record her aesthetic standards and views on contemporary trends, the picture that emerges is that of a literary statesman. Many writers, for instance, choose not to write reviews at all. Others prefer to review only those books they can praise. Godwin takes neither of these easy routes. Consider her commentary on Pat Conroy's novel *The Prince of Tides*. She describes Conroy as a "smart man and serious writer . . . waylaid by the bullying monster of heavy-handed, inflated plot and the siren voice of Mother South at her treacherous worst— embroidered, sentimental, inexact."[18]

Godwin is equally clear about what she does like in fiction. She says that her favorite writers are those who "wrote to discover, to work out, to test their ideas in the process of writing. As they worked on their novels, they worked on their lives: on their vision of life. They tested it, revised it, expanded it" ("Uses," 9). Thus, her definition of good writing brings us full circle to an awareness that life and fiction, reality and art, are for Godwin truly inseparable and that to try to separate them is the first step toward inferior work.

In "How to Be the Heroine of Your Own Life," Godwin opens by describing a scene reminiscent of the opening scene of *A Southern Family*, but the essay is about a real-life conversation between Godwin and her best friend, not about a fictional conversation between her alter ego Clare Campion and her friend Julia. As Godwin and her friend discuss their lives, the friend makes a comment that Godwin realizes is the key to making one-self the heroine of one's life. Her friend says, "We've been able to perceive what we've been going through *imaginatively,* rather than just suffering what happens to us emotionally" ("Heroine," 194). This distinction is pre-cisely the point that Joanne S. Frye makes about how Violet Clay is different from Godwin's previous heroines: Violet shapes her destiny, imaginatively and actively, instead of passively awaiting what will be.

If a single element of Godwin's growth as a writer is key to the continu-ing excellence of her work and to the expansion of her sensibilities and her technique, it is her recognition of the importance of immersing herself in the perspectives of others and her concomitant conviction that such immersion is impossible if one has not simultaneously been hyperaware of one's own experience and reactions to it. In "How to Be the Heroine" she says, "Noth-ing is lost on [the heroine of her own life]. She has come to understand that you have to recognize the design in your own being before you can contrib-ute anything of value to the larger design of your civilization" ("Heroine," 196–97).

When photographer Mark Morrow went to take pictures of Godwin for his book *Images of the Southern Writer,* she seized his camera and began in-structing him on how to pose, saying, as she did so, "I just like to know how the other person feels."[19] In "A Diarist on Diarists" she discusses how she went about moving outward from the closed world of self to engage sympa-thetically and empathetically with the larger world: "As I became less trapped in my universe of moods and recognized my likeness to other Peo-ple and other things in the universe-at-large, my [diary] entries began to in-clude more space. Now there are animals and flowers and sunsets in my diary, as well as other people's problems. As a rule, I complain less and de-scribe more; even my complaints I try to lace with memorable description" ("Diarist," 13). As she says in an essay called "Being on Everybody's Side," the writer must develop "powers of observation and understanding to create believable characters" ("Diarist," 14). Thus, the key to Godwin's growth as a writer is as simple and as complicated as that: observe and understand. The reward for careful, sympathetic observation is, according to Godwin, that "the more you respect and focus on the singular and the strange, the more you become aware of the universal and infinite" ("Intro," xvi).

She realized in her London journal that she wanted to write about the mysterious part that did not fit into the truth of prescribed schemes and also realized that her predilection for order and shapeliness might be her down-fall if she were not constantly aware of its potential for leading her away from the very truths she hoped to pursue. Eventually Godwin discovered that she must let her characters have the same freedom to shape their experience that she herself sought in both her life and her work. In an essay that discusses the origins and the evolution of her short story "Dream Children," Godwin describes through a religious analogy this crucial understanding of how characters work in fiction:

> I understood for the first time the *religious* nature of the relationship between an author and his characters in a novel. A novel is like a life. . . . And when I begin a novel, I must rough out a plan of this life. This is the part comparable to predestination. But then, on every page, at every turning point along the way, I must allow my character to alter, bend, and shape that destiny. That allowance on my part, that impetus on his, is the part comparable to free will.[20]

As she worked on *A Mother and Two Daughters*, the novel that took her from average sales of 8,000 or fewer on a novel to sales of 85,000 in hardcover and 1.5 million in paperback,[21] Godwin felt that "something in me was longing to leap that point-of-view barrier and be more than one person at a time."[22] Thus, she altered her usual method of narrating a novel and went against the advice of teachers and the current trend toward minimal narratives to write a huge, sprawling, old-fashioned sort of tale with a narrator who can enter into the perspective of almost anyone who passes through the scene. The sales figures for *A Mother and Two Daughters* demonstrate that this move to a less restrictive point of view, and the subsequent broadening of scope in material, connected Godwin to a much larger audience than she had previously enjoyed. The feeling of connectedness that emerges in her work in that novel, however, goes far beyond sales figures. For the author's effort to connect with her numerous characters, many of them quite different from herself, goes against the grain of the southern belle and the impulses that the southern-reared Godwin was trained to heed.[23] The connectedness of *A Mother and Two Daughters* and Godwin's subsequent work is the chief evidence that she is not merely a writer of the introverted, personal, self-absorbed story of a very specific sort of woman, a woman much like the author herself. She is not a writer bound too tightly by the autobiographical. She is, in fact, a writer whose career is a pattern of movement away from those limitations and toward work that "can affect other individuals and then society and the world."[24]

In a journal entry headed "Philosophy and Politics," dated 27 August 1987, Godwin writes, "I had a vision—from half-sleep—of People in a crowded place, milling around in some vast place like Penn Station. I have been brought up to believe that each person is *alone* in that crowd, but I now saw how, one day, they might all be connected and *know themselves connected*" ("Journals," 194). The shape and motion of that vision is perhaps the best metaphor for the shape and motion of Gail Godwin's career as a novelist. She is a writer shaped and informed by her specific past, writing toward a connection with the larger world, and through the act of writing and the artifacts produced, working to make the world more aware of itself and its universality.

Less than a week after she experienced this vision, Godwin dreamed that she was a candidate for political office and was being pressed to state her platform. She responded by saying, "Constructive sorrow. My platform is constructive sorrow" ("Journals," 195). Her body of work suggests that what she would construct from her realistic awareness of the sorrows of her own life and our larger, common life is art, stories working toward truth and quietly reasonable joy.

Chapter Two

The Perfectionists and *Glass People*: The Shape of Things to Come

Cameron Bolt, a protagonist of Godwin's second novel, *Glass People,* uses a political speech to articulate one of the controlling images of his personal vision. To Cameron, relationships—marriages, friendships, families—are containers, shapes, that we use as forms in which to store our individual identities. He acknowledges that there are "many, many combinations of container and contained. But the requisites are always the same."[1] Each element, in his metaphor, provides the other with "an underpinning of earned trust upon which it is possible to build new achievements" (*GP*, 99).

In many ways, *The Perfectionists* and *Glass People* are models for Godwin's concept of fiction as a container:

Of course there are good and bad containers. A container should not be too thick. Too rigid. Then the glass becomes cloudy, it becomes opaque to the needs of both sides, a blind prison wall. . . . But it can't be too thin, too flaccid, either. In that case, what is contained spills out into license, anarchy, chaos. Boundary lines are violated. (*GP*, 100)

Read as an interpretation of narrative technique, this statement by Cameron Bolt serves equally well to illuminate Godwin's theories of the relationship between novel and author-narrator, novel and reader, and author-narrator and reader. *The Perfectionists* and *Glass People* define basic qualities of Godwin's novels: theme, character, plot, and narrative strategy are all established in a way that remains the basis for her fiction. Godwin, though, realizes that shapes are much more fluid, organic, alive than Cameron Bolt believes. She also acknowledges more honestly and realistically our creative manipulation of these controlling patterns.

Both *The Perfectionists* and *Glass People* tell the story of an unhappy marriage. In both cases, the husband has an enormous power over his wife, who feels compelled to escape. Godwin's two shortest novels, each told from a limited third-person point of view (*Glass People* alternates between the wife's and the husband's perspectives), introduce an intelligent, allusive, analytical posture that permeates all her novels.

Although later novels feature unmarried female protagonists, the paradox persists of wanting male companionship and love, even male dominance, and, at the same time, wanting freedom and individual integrity. Godwin experiments with point of view in later novels—using first person, an old-fashioned omniscience, and modernist intercutting of multiple limited perspectives—but she never retreats from an essential question raised by the perspectives used in the early novels: how honest and complete is any approach to a story or to a single event within that story?

All of Godwin's main characters want to live their best life, as Jane Clifford puts it to her mother in *The Odd Woman*. Dane Tarrant Empson and Francesca Bolt, the youngest and the least emotionally complex of Godwin's heroines, want to find their best lives just as much as do their more mature and complex descendants, but, as the titles of their stories suggest, they are too idealistic and too fragile.

Dane Tarrant, a young American reporter, meets John Empson, a psychotherapist, while she is working in London. When *The Perfectionists* begins, they have been married 10 months, and Dane has given up her career. Traveling with Robin, John's son from an affair with a fellow medical student, and with Penelope MacMahon, one of John's patients, the Empsons are vacationing on the island of Majorca. Ironically, the get-away increases tension in the Empsons' marriage rather than providing escape and helping dissolve their unhappiness. The pattern of dislocating characters, drawing them out of their natural environment—or, in some cases, forcing them to return to their "natural" but abandoned environment—is important to the foundation of Godwin's fictive world. In *Glass People*, Francesca, the wife, goes on holiday alone, and in subsequent novels funerals are often the impetus for the trips that characters take.

An Island Getaway

The exotic and beautiful island setting of Majorca is at first glance a romantic one, but beneath this idyllic exterior Dane Empson senses rigidity. She sees a group of Spanish women leaving mass, and she immediately divides them into three categories: young and virginal, with white missals and fresh skin; married and pregnant; or old and widowed, dressed in funereal black: "She envied them their definitive stages of womanhood. It was all done for them. They had only to flow along with nature's seasons, being

courted, bedded, bechilded, and bereaved. There were not all those inter-
stices of ambition and neurosis for them to fall into."[2] Dane's surprising
covetousness of such a bound existence not only prefigures the significant
role of a shaped, contained life, but also introduces one of the major conflicts to be faced by Godwin's cast of female characters over the course of
eight novels and two collections of short stories.

Dane is typical of Godwin's female protagonists in several other important ways. Her desire for a safe, programmed life is in direct conflict with
her longing for a transcendent existence in which she feels neither con-
stricted nor pressured, alone nor invaded. She has goals for her personal life
so unrealistic and idealistic as to make her a perfectionist, and perfectionists
are doomed to disappointment in the real world.

The obstacles facing Dane are also typical of those faced by Godwin's
protagonists in general. The need to gain the approval of others without
giving oneself over to them automatically produces friction, and Dane travels with three others on this journey for which she has such high hopes. In
addition, she is an avid observer, a collector of other people's stories, which
she then uses to measure and evaluate her own life.

Trying on Others' Lives

Penelope MacMahon, John Empson's patient who travels with the couple, is the first of the women against whom Dane measures herself; she
serves as a reminder of what single life is like for a young woman, and
Penelope's affair with Karl Heykoop complicates Dane's views of sexuality,
marriage, and friendship.

When they arrive in Majorca, Penelope is thrilled by the open, greedy
looks of the Majorcan men, who are unafraid to exhibit their desire and who
are, thus, a refreshing change from the Englishmen Penelope is used to.
Dane realizes that the Majorcans' lusty looks that Penelope relishes as sexual
bravado, as promises of adventures to come, have another side. Once married, once possessed, so to speak, that tantalizing desire becomes oppres-
sively demanding. Men—specifically John and Robin in Dane's life—
demand constant emotional and physical nurturing.

The pressure of having a relative stranger along on a family vacation is
obvious. That Dane, John, and Robin are not a long-established and traditionally structured family makes the pressure even more intense. But the
greatest pressure comes from Penelope's idealized view of John and Dane
and their marriage. As is the case with almost all of Godwin's protagonists,
Dane is well aware of Penelope's image of her and feels considerable respon-

sibility to live up to it. When Penelope also idealizes Dane's relationship with Robin, she adds yet another role to the list of expectations Dane feels compelled to fulfill.

There is a terrible ambiguity about this relationship between perceiver and perceived, and it is clearly one of Godwin's major concerns as a fiction writer. Dane does not see herself, her marriage, or her relationship with her stepson in the same way that Penelope does, but she wants to believe in what her companion sees and therefore attempts to create the Dane that Penelope sees. Instead of relaxing on vacation, she finds herself working hard to measure up to the role someone else has written for her. At the same time, like most Godwin protagonists, she is perpetually concerned with herself as defined from within.

In part, Dane tries to be true to herself by undercutting Penelope's romantic view of men and marriage with wisdom drawn from her 10 months' experience. When Penelope laments the loneliness of single life, Dane argues for its freedom, and the richness of its possibilities.

Once Penelope has become involved with Karl Heykoop and Dane has met his wife, Polly, and discovered that Karl's behavior with Penelope is but another repetition in a long cycle of infidelity, she feels tempted to force the younger woman to face the facts:

She saw herself knocking briskly at the girl's door, going in and lifting the whole thing to a tone of dry sarcasm against the world of ridiculous men. ("What do you expect, Penelope? They're all such children. Get all the experience you can from him. It will help you manipulate your future ones.") (*P*, 134)

Despite these impulses toward truth and reality, with Penelope as with everyone else, Dane justifies her role-playing philosophy by remembering William James and his belief that "if you acted the part long enough you became the real thing" (*P*, 33). The most extreme example of this behavior is perhaps Dane's interaction with an Englishwoman who is staying at the Empsons' hotel. Mrs. Hart, seeing Dane struggle with Robin, comes forward to give her some simple advice about motherhood: the child needs his beach shoes on to keep his feet from burning on the hot walkway and the beach sand.

Mrs. Hart is gentle and kind, not judgmental or condescending. Dane, filled with guilt about forgetting the shoes and about her ambivalent feelings toward her stepson, decides that she must be the young mother that Mrs. Hart was and would want her to be. She works out a fantasy involving Mrs. Hart and the story of her marriage—an oddly contrived situation in which she marries a much older man because he needs her and because he asks her, after she refuses his proposal, to do him one last favor and select the materials for redecorating his home. She cannot do the favor and then not see the things she has selected in their proper place.

Mrs. Hart's marriage stands not for a union of love but for other things —history, commitment, understanding, exchange, and children. Dane uses parts of this story in a sexual fantasy while she is making love with John; that is, she *becomes* Mrs. Hart, takes on the feelings of her repressed Victorian marriage, in order to reach a higher state of arousal with John. She also creates an imaginary pregnancy for herself in order to gain Mrs. Hart's most complete approval, for to the older woman, children are the reason for marriage, the source of all happiness.

The most involved and unsettling of Dane's encounters with other women takes place when she has created for herself an afternoon escape from John and Robin. After going into a church and briefly contemplating her mother's departure from marriage to Dane's father, a military man who collected shoes for the weekly polishing ritual while his wife and another man packed belongings into the car that would take her away from him and his daughter, Dane walks through the village resolving to try harder to transform her relationships with John and Robin.

Immediately after she reaches this new resolve, she comes upon Polly Heykoop, who is spanking her children with obvious relish and enormous release and who makes a general announcement to the world as she finishes: "It's too fucking much" (*P*, 100). Drawn to this scene as if she were "entering an interesting book" (*P*, 101), Dane approaches this vibrant stranger with applause, endorsing the woman's actions and her sentiments.

The encounter serves to undercut the romantic, idealistic oath Dane has just sworn and forces her to cut through such fantasy to practical truth. Polly offers Dane a chance for real connection, a relationship beyond role playing and destructive second-guessing, but Dane decides to impress Polly rather than confide in her. She makes a long poetic speech about her marriage, turning it into an ideal of the modern, self-conscious, and complex marriage that she thought she and John would have but which she now resents in the imperfect state to which they have evolved. In fact, their marriage has turned out so badly, Dane finds herself regressing to the older ideal of the Victorian marriage, with its dignity and form (another foreshadowing of Cameron Bolt and the theory of containers), its respect for privacy and for putting the best foot forward—Mrs. Hart's story.

When the Empsons, Robin, and Penelope go to the Heykoops' house for lunch, Dane is very aware of the role playing going on between Karl and

Polly, and she sees Penelope as a willing object for both of them. The obvious maneuvering and dishonesty repulse her, not so much because of her emotional involvement with any of these people but because she makes the connection between what the Heykoops are doing and what she and John are doing.

The similarity is reinforced by Penelope's being the outsider who has entered the world of each marriage. Her involvement with Karl is, of course, sexual, and we have no information that suggests that she and John are sexually involved. But Penelope is a third party on the Empsons' vacation, and Dane experiences an odd sense of deja vu when John's conversation with Penelope in the hotel dining room is a replay of his first conversation with her. There is nothing overtly sexual about the subject matter—John's resonance theory of extrasensory perception—but the Empson marriage is not the primitive, sexual bond that the Heykoops' is. Dane and John are linked by something more mystical, and his seduction of Dane was cerebral, not genital. To see him perform the same "routine" for Penelope suggests that there is a parallel to Karl's overtly sexual seduction of the same woman.

Finally, Dane cannot be the friend that Polly Heykoop wants. Her failure—or her choice—is partly the result of her strong sense of being herself "with as few concessions as possible" (*P*, 115). To agree to "complete" Polly would be an admission that she herself might also need completing and require outside help to be a whole person. In addition, as she argues to Polly, Dane truly believes that the completing function that Polly describes is the role of a mate, not of a friend.

When Polly counters that husbands and wives cannot analyze relationships, at least not their own, together without destroying the magical, unknowable part of themselves that allows their connection, their romance, to flourish or at least to survive, Dane finds herself resorting again to the kind of thinking that she finds repulsive in her husband. As she tells Polly that complex humans are limitless and always retain their mystery and otherness, she realizes that she is echoing John and is taking his side of an argument they themselves might have.

Dane's rejection of the deeper connection Polly desires is, in part, her last retreat into a false image of herself. One way to measure the growth of Godwin's protagonists in later books is to observe that the later characters most often eventually confront the sorts of situations that Dane retreats from, even though they almost always share her reservations about such naked revelations of the self.

The other woman who plays a large part in Dane's vacation is an unnamed French woman who is, in Dane's eyes, an ideal made real. The two women never exchange a word. The French woman remains an unexamined, unpossessed ideal and thus retains her mythic charm and attraction. The French woman and her husband are vacationing with their two small children. They are cool, sleek, and handsome, and to Dane they have an ideal harmony, a unity, that she envies. Even when she and John tour the French couple's accommodations after John decides they might extend the vacation and Dane sees that they are cramped and definitely unglamorous, she still maintains the idealized version of the French woman's story.

This concept is reiterated when Dane tries to comfort Penelope about Karl. She tells the girl that she, not Polly Heykoop, has the best of the deal because Penelope will have her unsullied image of Karl to carry away with her. The unpossessed ideal can be "eternally fascinating" (*P*, 143); the possessed man will be an inevitable letdown.

Getting Your Man—and His Child

The dilemma of the woman who gets what she wants—her man—is at the heart of *The Perfectionists*. The relationships with other women are demonstrations of Dane's tendency to try on others' lives through actual knowledge or through her imagination, much as someone would try on clothes. She is looking for a story that fits, that is flattering and comfortable. Penelope's loneliness and desperation, Mrs. Hart's loveless, dutiful marriage of form and order, and Polly's cynical primitivism make Dane alternately uncomfortable, envious, and falsely secure, while the unsullied image of the French woman hovers in the back of her mind to remind her that she is not what she wants to be. But all these characters and all their stories are used structurally to develop and enrich the main story, that of Dane's relationship with her husband.

One aspect of Dane's attraction to John Empson is a very traditional desire for security, a desire that most of Godwin's female protagonists at least flirt with. John is not a traditionally heroic figure. He is small and pale, slightly crippled, and not at all handsome in any conventional sense. His teeth are bad. What attracts Dane and leads her to believe that he can satisfy her longing for shelter is the power of his mind and, perhaps, what Dane imagines or perceives to be his spirit.

Making John a psychotherapist (the profession of Godwin's second husband) is crucial to the plot and to the development of Dane's character: "He had that rare talent of explaining people to themselves, computerizing their shadowy miasmas in his great brain and handing them back a neat card on which their secrets and fears had been programmed into a coherent, less threatening shape" (*P,* 8). From her childhood with her military father, Dane learned that order is an antidote to the chaos that invades life without warning. Despite the heady idealism suggested in her initial reactions to John, the fantasy Dane engages in is one of marriage—the most traditional, confining shape into which one might try to fit.

After they first meet, John does not communicate with Dane for three weeks, during which time her image of him as the possible vehicle for the ideal life she longs for builds within her. At first his silence allows her to consider his flaws. Then she is hurt by inattention from such a flawed creature and uses the flaws to assuage her pain. Finally, when enough time passes, she begins to idealize the man in order to justify his reasons for ignoring her. When a letter comes three weeks later, his invitation is not to dinner or a movie. He asks Dane to share the universe with him.

With some variation in time frame and the expectations and participation of the female character, this pattern persists through Godwin's next two novels—the woman creates an image of a man she has met and is then separated from. She then obtains the man attached to the image she has created and finds herself wondering what to do. Not until *Violet Clay* does Godwin begin a novel with a protagonist getting rid of the man in her life and getting about the business of what John Empson advises Dane to do early on: to sort out what she's for and what she's against and to live by that.

Dane cannot do what John says because she cannot resolve the paradox inherent in her goal. She wants to "find the reality [that will be] greater than the dream" (*P,* 29), meaning that she wants to live a life composed of daily events and populated by people that *exceed* the life of her imagination, her dream life. The problem is further complicated by the false nature of part of the ideal Dane sets up from the very beginning. When John proposes to her, she looks into the "terrible brown intensity" of his eyes and believes that all she wants at this point is "to complete her self-abnegation to the will of this determined man" (*P,* 67).

John correctly identifies Dane as a "soul on the prowl" (*P,* 57) and agrees to help her toward the complete understanding of self in relation to the universe that she believes him to possess. He has known her only a very short time, and Dane has made a point of presenting to him an image to which she thinks he will respond favorably. Thus, he has no way to know what an overwhelming and impossible task he is agreeing to undertake.

John also sees himself as far less complete and powerful than Dane believes him to be. In fact, his unfinished quality is the source of strength and power for him. She finds herself frustrated that she cannot define for herself and for others who or what John is, but she also realizes that her feeling of having been deceived about him comes from "her own false assumptions." She has to acknowledge that "John had never pretended to be anything but his strange nebulous self" (P, 40).

One of the main demands that strange self makes of his partner is that she accept his faults and weaknesses and help him to confront and deal with them. Obviously, this trait is in direct conflict with Dane's need for an ideal partner. After they are married, John's displays of needfulness begin to repulse Dane. She does not, she believes, require that he be invulnerable, but she does wish that he did not so proudly display his needs and weaknesses and that he would not try to force her to participate in his efforts to confront and grow beyond them.

An incident that occurs while they are vacationing illustrates the different perspectives Dane and John have toward his "growth" experiences. On a walk through a forest alone, John undergoes a profound moment with a "mothering" tree. He falls asleep beneath the tree and has a powerful dream. According to his interpretation, the tree represents his earthly, individual life while the moon overhead symbolizes a great cosmic force. These two forces battle for possession of John, and when the tree wins, he ejaculates. Thus, he reads the dream as an affirmation of his real self—his earthly life of growth toward a larger self. When he shares this intensely significant experience with Dane, the literal image of her husband, frail and crippled, ejaculating beneath a tree sickens her. The symbolic import is lost in the repulsive nature of the literal image.

The messiness, literal and symbolic, that this experience and John and Dane's conflict over it embody suggests the fundamental conflict in their approaches to life. Dane, partly as a result of her childhood with her father, is obsessed with order while John distinguishes between general messiness and the natural disorder that leads to growth. John's concept of marriage is that it should extend the partners, not restrict them, and he feels that Dane's response to his gladly offered piece of himself is restricting rather than nurturing.

Dane seems to conclude that transcendence is impossible in their relationship because John is human. Therefore, she will settle for, in fact barter sex for, a John who is capable of bringing order and control to her life. But even in sex, they work toward opposite goals. Dane seeks oblivion while John, eyes wide open at all times, seeks a hyperconscious state in which he is even more painfully aware than usual of everything going on within and around him.

Because Dane is not yet ready to challenge John directly or to sever completely their bond, the child, Robin, becomes both a double for Dane in his conflict with his father and a surrogate for John as an outlet for Dane's hostilities and frustrations. Dane concludes that "She was about as motherly as a stone and about as concerned about it as one" (*P,* 162). Thus, if John's motive in marrying her was to acquire a mother figure for his son—and for the child within him, those "tender shoots" of himself—Dane recognizes that she is not suited for the role he has assigned her.

She determines to force Robin into a junior comradeship of sorts. Her projecting of her needs in regard to her husband onto his child is reinforced by John's own insistence on the close identification between him and his son. John forces her to accept and deal with him and Robin on the assumption that Robin *is* John as a child. Thus, the adult wife is forced to deal with a grown man, her husband, as if he were a child and a hostile child at that. John takes an obvious psychological truth and forces Dane to interpret it literally. When Robin refuses to speak to her, she then must feel like a failure at communicating with John-as-child, which the adult John desires.

When Dane takes Robin swimming, she forces him to make a choice. He can enjoy the pleasures of the water by staying attached to Dane, or he can separate from her, stay on the beach, and sacrifice the sensual pleasure of swimming. He reluctantly chooses to swim with Dane holding him in her arms, but he will not acknowledge that she is the agent of his physical pleasure.

Gradually, Dane begins to sense a power in Robin's impassivity. Her admiration for his autonomy is strengthened when she watches him rebel against just the sort of order and direction in their lives that she herself desires from John. When the father orders the son to dress himself and to comb his own hair, Robin refuses, and Dane finds herself taking his side and helping him to perform the tasks. Her alignment with Robin begins to suggest that she is taking her first step away from John.

During an evening of dancing with the Heykoops and Penelope in a bar, Dane decides to play Robin. She remains entirely silent and experiences the power of that silence. Others are forced to interpret it, which they usually do "according to their own guilts and needs" (*P,* 188). John forces her to dance with him, and their awkwardness, especially as she compares it to the fluidity of the French couple, convinces her that they will never learn to move together without snarling.

To emphasize further the serious sexual estrangement that is at the heart of the marital problems, Godwin has Dane go home from the failure at dancing with John and take Robin into bed with her. Thus, she chooses her surrogate-antagonist, the child rather than the man. The next day she refuses John's invitation to swim and gets into a physical fight with Robin. She draws blood, imagines sucking the breath from him. This action brings her a "pure, perfect peace" as Robin's eyes "hardened against her in a decision far beyond their years" (*P*, 211). Dane seeks cosmic experience by almost killing Robin. Symbolically, this suggests that she must kill John, separate from him, in order to survive, much less to have the *un*ordinary life that is her deepest desire.

Intensity without Guidance

Early in the novel John is writing in his journal, and Penelope asks Dane what he is writing. Dane replies that it has something to do with an idea John has had about "Heraclitus and Jung's concept on enantiodromia." Dane paraphrases the idea this way: "Overcoming your contradictions on a given level, you can swing wider, into the next level of growth" (*P*, 39). Dane claims not to understand this concept, and it is this lack of understanding that prevents her from experiencing the growth typical of Godwin's other protagonists.

The ironic diminishing of Dane's struggle as the focus shifts to her conflict with Robin as well as her increasing identification with the child suggests that she, like John, is too unfinished, too immature, to be a comrade, an imperfect equal. The concern with preserving and asserting the self, the integrity of the ego, in a character like Dane is, finally, adolescent behavior. In her sixth novel, *The Finishing School,* Godwin uses an adolescent protagonist for the first time. But because the novel is told in first person, by the adult Justin Stokes looking back on the events of her fourteenth summer, even Justin has more irony about herself and her motives than Dane does. Without that ironic perspective, Dane remains an unsatisfying character, and her struggle cannot be satisfactorily resolved.

The important question raised by Godwin's treatment of Dane Empson is the relationship between protagonist and narrator. In the end, it is not clear enough where the author-narrator separates from Dane and her perceptions, flawed and unresolved though they are. Thus, the reader cannot clearly determine what the novel's intentions are in terms of thematic statement. Is Dane a better or a worse character at novel's end? Happier or more depressed? Stronger or weaker? Is it better to compromise an ideal and settle for ordinary, or is it better to hold fast to ideals and the concomitant possibility, indeed likelihood, of disillusionment and defeat? In *The Perfectionists* the characters are too emotionally involved with the issues that raise these questions to provide acceptable answers. The narrator does not maintain enough distance from her characters to do so. Thus, the experience of reading this first novel is one of being drawn into scenes and situations of enormous intensity without receiving enough guidance on how to interpret them.

People Who Live in Glass Marriages . . .

The intercutting of two perspectives—those of wife and husband—that Godwin uses in *Glass People* perhaps suggests that the ambiguities of situation and character are less than in *The Perfectionists*. Clearly, the author-narrator will be positioned differently with regard to at least one of the characters whose points of view are presented.

In *Glass People* there is a greater distance between narrator and character in the sections of the novel told from Cameron Bolt's perspective than there is in *The Perfectionists* between the narrator and Dane. Even in the portions of the story told from Francesca's point of view, the feeling of narrative attachment to character is less. This is in part a result of the Bolts' being both less realistic and less emotionally intense characters than the Empsons. The Bolts have not set out to discover the universe's secret messages to them.

Cameron Bolt is much more likely to impose his messages on the universe or to try to do so. His theory of shapes is a perfect example of how he sees his personal vision as a means for clarifying and improving the universe that he inhabits. His wife Francesca, on the other hand, seems utterly disinclined to heed the universe at all.

Yet the Bolts find themselves in a marriage that does have similarities to the Empsons'. Francesca Bolt's resentment of her husband's power is deeper and more long-standing than Dane Empson's negative attitude toward her husband, but Francesca has been married longer than Dane, too.

Like Dane, Francesca takes a trip described as a vacation, but it becomes a trial separation from her husband, a last desperate effort to develop and assert a strong individual identity before she is completely subsumed by the role her husband designs for her. Because she travels alone and, during the course of her journey, takes on work and tries to construct an independent life, Francesca is a character who appears to present a less ambiguous solution than her predecessor to the problems of dissatisfaction in marriage and the slow erosion of female identity within relationships dominated by powerful male figures.

Like *The Perfectionists*, *Glass People* ends with the female protagonist's having failed to attain the goal she sets for herself when she undertakes her journey. The plot of *Glass People* brings Francesca back to California and back to Cameron, putting her well-being and her growth back in his hands, at least temporarily, so there is still a measure of ambiguity about how a woman who longs to live her best life can best set about accomplishing that goal. However, the attitude that both Francesca and the novel's narrator take toward this resolution and the failure to reach the original goal of separating from Cameron has an irony missing in *The Perfectionists*. Through Francesca, Godwin suggests that even a weak woman has powers beyond those of a powerful man and that if she learns to use those powers to manipulate her life much as novelists manipulate characters and events, she can attain success of a different order than she originally imagined. Francesca's ironic triumph is presented in mythic rather than realistic terms, but it opens the way that Godwin's later protagonists follow to more realistic, more convincing triumphs.

An Unfinished Woman

The unmarried Francesca has goals very similar to those Dane Empson has before marriage: "It's as though I want some final force to enter me and take over my body, set me on some genuine destiny that can't be changed, that I can't turn back from" (*GP*, 13).

Like Dane, she is very young when she marries. As her identity evolves, she begins to revise her goals, to rebel, and to try on the identities of other characters almost as if she were shopping for clothes (a metaphor Godwin uses several times in her novels and short stories). Examining role models is, of course, a valid way of developing one's identity, but Francesca seems to believe that she will be able to discover an identity that she can lift whole cloth and drop over herself. Thus, after an effort that verges on the heroic, if naive, Francesca finds herself in a department store with Cameron, who literally buys her the identity of his choosing.

Francesca is much less desperate, focused, and energetic in her quest for identity than Dane. Although the demands of marriage have left Dane mentally and spiritually exhausted, Francesca finds herself in a marriage that makes absolutely no demands on her. Cameron is a district attorney in California. Professionally powerful and ambitious, he is also a perfect and willing househusband. He does all the chores—the shopping, the cooking, everything. All he asks of his wife is that she be her incredibly beautiful self. So Francesca sleeps most of the time. If beauty is all that is required of one, beauty sleep can legitimately become a primary occupation.

Francesca becomes pregnant by the novel's end, but there is a great deal of irony associated with her becoming a mother. No subsequent Godwin protagonist will allow maternity to be the answer in her search for identity. Thus, Francesca virtually completes Godwin's exploration of the idiom of identity-through-reproduction, and the ironies of her pregnancy suggest that Godwin does not see reproduction itself as a valid way toward defining an independent and evolving self. It is more Francesca's ability to *use* the pregnancy than the actual fact of her expecting a baby that Godwin posits as a key to independence and personal power.

Although we know almost nothing of Dane's sexual background prior to her meeting John, Godwin does indicate that Francesca's experience prior to Cameron had been disappointing. At their early meetings, through her stepfather, Jonathan, Francesca is aloof, and Cameron finds her beautiful but formidable, a challenge. For her part, Francesca begins to wonder if Cameron's self-restraint could be the beginning of passion. She practices the power of silence (as Dane does when she decides to "play Robin" in *The Perfectionists*) and does not deal with him as she would her disappointing lovers. When Cameron finally touches her, makes sensual contact, she is not disappointed.

Immediately after she experiences this new, powerful sensation, Cameron is called back to California on business. Instead of going home, Francesca waits for him at the mountain cabin he has rented. She snoops among his things, eats his food, drinks his wine, sleeps in his bed wearing his shirt. When she awakens from a beautiful woman's worst nightmare—she has no reflection; no one, including herself, can *see* her, and thus she has no identity —Cameron is miraculously there to "save" her, to see her. So she marries him, imagining that her destiny has found her.

Francesca's background is in part responsible for her being the kind of woman who would marry a man after such a romanticized and unexamined relationship because he saves her from a nightmare. Much more than Dane, Francesca is a character who suggests what evolves into a major Godwin theme—the inescapable role of family life in shaping an individual's sense of self.

Francesca's childhood is lush with indulgence. Brought up in an unspecified mountainous region of the South (very similar to the more specific Mountain City, North Carolina, that is home to several later Godwin protagonists), Francesca lives with her mother and father until her father's death when she is 18. He apparently leaves his wife and daughter well provided for if they are careful, plan ahead, and live realistically. Kate, her mother, and Francesca, however, become best friends. They travel and spend money. Their extravagance draws them closer to each other and separates them from their small, conservative community, whose citizens see their spending and traveling as frivolous and disrespectful of the dead husband and father.

Another way in which Godwin makes Francesca's past significant is to keep the mother-daughter relationship alive in the time present of the story. When Cameron and Francesca decide that she should take a vacation in order to restore her energy and bring her back to life, they agree that she should go to visit Kate. But the lassitude that has taken over Francesca's soul has affected even that connection. She and Kate have not been in contact for over a year, and when she does reach her mother and get her to agree to the visit, Francesca arrives to find a completely new Kate.

Her return to Kate may, at first, be an attempt to escape, but her mother's inability to fulfill the role of familiar haven forces Francesca to face two obvious alternatives: routine or escape. Like Dane, who faces similarly limited options, Francesca finds that her present reality makes both untenable, and she must begin to look around her for guides to a better life.

Francesca's effort to connect with her mother and to draw from Kate's current life something that will be useful in creating a new, happier Francesca and her effort to reconcile the conflict in her mind between the old Kate and the one she meets on this trip make Francesca's struggle to define her own identity more complex and difficult than Dane's. This task of working out her relationship with Kate is only one indication that *Glass People* is a more complicated and richer novel than *The Perfectionists,* though its simpler language and its less analytical protagonist might at first suggest the reverse.

The Kate who allowed Francesca to sleepwalk through life no longer exists. Following the death of her second husband, the mysteriously wealthy Jonathan, Kate has had to awaken from her own fantasy. Without Jonathan, the money disappears; his wealth was apparently a very fragile structure, an illusion kept intact by the force of Jonathan's personality.

What Francesca finds when she gets to her mother's house is a woman who has abandoned makeup, high fashion, and her spectacular mountain fortress for a small cabin and a salt-of-the-earth man named Ware Smith. The new Kate eats vegetables grown in their garden and drinks herbal teas. She is also pregnant, and, worst of all for Francesca, she is oddly distant. The mother of her past was also her friend and confidante. The new Kate spends much of her time behind the closed door of the bedroom she shares with Ware.

When Francesca does manage to have a conversation with her mother about the drastic changes in her life, Kate explains that she and Ware made their decision to be together out of mutual need rather than out of some more romantic ideal of love. Each had tried independence and found it lonely and difficult. Francesca does notice that, despite the changed environment, her mother has been able to engender in Ware the same pride and worship that she had instilled in Francesca's father and Jonathan. Apparently she does so by being the woman that Ware needs her to be—dressed in flannel, hair in braids, swollen with his child.

The woman Cameron Bolt needs is very different, but the image of her mother that Francesca draws from her oddly disappointing visit provides key elements of the self Francesca will eventually create and allow Cameron to use for his own purposes. She carries from the visit, perhaps unconsciously, a message about the irony of attaining power for the self through playing a role created by another. The other women who play a part in Francesca's exploration of her identity have a less lasting impact on the ultimate version of self Francesca arrives at than does Kate. Through her relationships with Nina Brett, whom she meets at an employment agency, M Evans, for whom she works as an amanuensis, and an unseen woman in the hotel room adjoining hers, Francesca learns little about who she can be, but a great deal about who and what she cannot.

After her week with Kate in the mountains, Francesca feels revitalized. In the airport on her way back to California, she meets a man and has a brief affair. One result of the encounter is that she decides to stay in New York and get a job, although she cannot tell Cameron the whole truth about her decision. She tells him that she is staying in New York to do some shopping for the new fall fashions.

When she goes to an employment agency in search of a job, Francesca meets Nina Brett, and, for the first time in her life, her image in the mirror seems insufficient when she compares it to her image of Ms. Brett. The epitome of a cool, urban professional woman of the early 1970s, Nina Brett quickly informs Francesca that she is qualified for almost nothing.

Francesca's desperation increases when she returns to the shabby hotel where she has taken rooms to avoid using money Cameron sends after she has decided to leave him. The maid tells Francesca about another woman, a long-term guest, Mrs. King, who is entirely helpless. She cannot open and heat a can of soup. Since the death of her husband, the hotel staff has taken over the task of tending her.

Her terror at the possibility of being Mrs. King leads Francesca to M Evans, the next of her models in the quest to create a self. An intimidating hulk of a woman, M has recently shaved her head as part of her ongoing effort to rid herself of her past identity. Francesca finds her hair among the other items of clutter and refuse that dominate her apartment. Too busy with the work to which she has committed her new life—developing a blueprint for a Desirable World—M Evans has also dropped her name from the past, which she refers to as her contingent life. Thelma becomes simply M: "It's my posthumous name. It stands for me, the pure, uncluttered, anonymous me. I have died to the world for all practical purposes and now I am trying to become anonymous, transparent" (GP, 143).

After her respite in the mountains, Francesca has determined that she is finally ready to engage the world. She bravely calls in response to M's *Village Voice* advertisement for an amanuensis and ironically finds herself confronting a woman who seeks to be exactly what Francesca most fears being: anonymous and transparent. An additional irony comes from the fact that the tasks that M expects of her amanuensis are tasks that Francesca has not performed, even for herself. Cameron has done for her all the things that she must now do for M.

Part of Francesca's fascination with M and with her "job" as her amanuensis comes from the simple pleasure of accomplishing something. But perhaps the more important reason for Francesca to pursue the relationship is that M is a woman with an analytical mind, and she is willing to apply her skills of analysis to Francesca and to share with her "employee" the results. Since neither her nature nor her conditioning has encouraged the analytical side of Francesca, she must rely on someone else to train her in the ways of self-exploration. Whether M is a reliable guide is a serious question and one so obvious that even Francesca asks it. But reliability aside, she is the only guide available to Francesca, and she must use her.

Francesca's relationship with M is also an important link to her husband. M's plan for a Desirable World is similar to Cameron's design for society. It questions the need for remaking the existing world. When she describes Cameron's plan to M, Francesca makes him sound very much like John and Dane Empson, like a perfectionist: "It's as if there's a perfect one of everything in his world and he keeps checking the real thing against his own private ones" (GP, 157).

This instance of genuine insight by Francesca is a direct by-product of her contact with M, and she pursues it even further by considering the nature of those who are "artists of the ideal" (GP, 169). She decides that they are probably all selfish, as M is, that selfishness is inherent in the nature of their pursuit. Thus, by extension, Cameron is selfish, but the flaw is part of a larger package that involves his genuine desire to make a better world.

While she lies sick in bed waiting for her lover's phone call on Thursday of her first week in New York, Francesca is confronted with two separate mythic images of woman. In a magazine she half-heartedly reads, she finds an article about a bold new woman, unafraid to assert herself, full of energy and drive "toward her own unique destiny" (*GP,* 174). But Francesca cannot see the triumph that the new woman's eyes are focused on in the magazine illustration. She is too closely linked with the other mythic image Godwin weaves through this climactic scene.

For several days Francesca has been aware of the woman next door with whom she shares a bath. That woman, never seen in the novel, seems to be ill and spends all her time making phone calls and speaking in a foreign language, weeping, and being sick in the bathroom. On this Thursday evening, as she reads the magazine and waits for her phone to ring, Francesca hears the weeping and the trips to the bathroom again and considers offering to help. Unable to decide how to approach the task, she stays in her room contemplating the image of "women in rooms alone, weeping, waiting" (*GP,* 169). The horrible thought of Mrs. King, the helpless widow above her, also enters her consciousness, and just as the phone call that she has so eagerly awaited comes through, her own body betrays her. She is forced to hang up on her lover and run for the bathroom, where she becomes the woman she has pitied. The situation is made even more terrible when that woman has the courage to do what Francesca couldn't: she comes to the door of the shared bathroom to ask whether Francesca is all right.

In much the same way that Dane measures herself against the unnamed French woman, Francesca comes to gauge the chances for her success as an independent woman against her image of this other unnamed foreign woman. When she actually takes on the stranger's illness, the loneliness, the weeping, she is at her lowest point (*GP,* 173). By accepting a defeated image of herself, she makes herself ripe for Cameron's reappearance. She believes she is a failure at creating her own identity.

The Fragile Hero Flies to the Rescue

Francesca uses a lover, Mike, whom she meets in an airport, as a form of escape, but she also sees him as a more manageable male than Cameron, one less likely to consume her identity into his own powerful self. In that sense, Mike serves much the same function in *Glass People* that Robin serves in *The Perfectionists.* Of course, Mike is an adult, and the relationship between him and Francesca is clearly sexual in ways that Dane's relationship with Robin is not. Still, Mike is an effort on Francesca's part to succeed in a way that she knows she cannot with Cameron, and as with Dane's efforts with Robin, the outcome is finally more negative than positive.

Near the end of her visit with Kate, as she sunbathes nude and indulges

in a fantasy love affair, Francesca sees a snake. The obvious Freudian implications of this experience are examined in a fairly heavy-handed manner
that recalls D. H. Lawrence, but the important point is that Francesca is
frightened away from a wholehearted embracing of her fantasy life. On the
night after she sees the snake, she has a nightmare about returning to
Cameron, thus linking him with the snake and interfering with the new, imaginative life she pursues in the forest.

The terror of seeing the snake coupled with the nightmare about
Cameron and Kate's parting warning that some women need a man and
having one "is nothing to sneeze at" (GP, 69) might have been enough to
scare Francesca straight back to Cameron without any further effort to explore her identity. In the airport, however, she meets Mike and immediately
recognizes his face as the previously unidentified face of her fantasy lover.
With Mike, Francesca makes an effort to create her own destiny, one might
say, or she may be, like Dane in her relationship with Robin, avoiding direct
confrontation with her ambivalent sexual feelings about her husband
through a relationship with a less threatening partner.

By wedding the image of the fantasy lover who frees her long-frozen pas-
sions to this ordinary businessman, taken by her great beauty, just as other
men, including Cameron, have been, Francesca makes a critical error in the
universe that Gail Godwin writes about. She connects the ideal to the real
and is thus doomed to failure and disappointment. Mike is nothing more or
less than an ordinary man.

He is a false goal, but inadvertently, out of his own limitations, he urges
her toward what she originally set as her new goal, the most clearly defined
and admirable of her life. Francesca's obsession with Mike also serves to
broaden her understanding of Cameron's feelings for her. Like her husband
who cannot bear for her to hear him using the bathroom, she becomes
afraid that her humanity, having to perform the basic bodily functions, will
turn her lover against her. By playing her old courting games and letting
Mike order for her in a Greek restaurant, Francesca is pretending not to
have spent considerable time in Greece and not to know Greek menus quite
well. The pretense is in a way an acknowledgment that her husband, too,
might take pleasure in selecting her pleasures.

When Mike leaves, Francesca searches the hotel room to find some trace
of him, some evidence of his existence in her life, and comes across a bar of
soap still wet from his shower. Her reaction is very similar to Cameron's intense physical reaction to Francesca's garments that hang in their California
closet: "The small bar of soap was still wet. She picked it up and smelled it.
It was all she had of him" (GP, 94). But the absence of the real man fuels

her passion, just as Cameron's passion is fueled by the garments he takes from the closet and caresses. When she tries to explain to Mike why she prefers him to Cameron, it is significant that her hair falls in front of him and obscures his face, so that the thing she prefers to her real husband is again a faceless image, a fantasy lover.

Glass People is different from *The Perfectionists* in that the married couple whose conflict is at the heart of the novel are separated almost at the outset. One result of having the story take place in separate locations, each with its very different perspective, is that the tensions of daily contact so pervasive in the earlier novel disappear. Another effect of having Francesca and Cameron developed largely in isolation from each other is that the attitudes of each toward the other are presumably more straightforward and honest because the need for role playing and for editing thoughts and actions disappears.

The Cameron we see through Francesca's eyes is not entirely negative. Very early she thinks, "Whatever else he is not, he is moral, he is dutiful" (*GP,* 8–9), and although these are not necessarily qualities to inspire high romance, they are not traits easy to dismiss in a husband either.

Nor is Cameron incapable of passion. Presented from Francesca's point of view, their first physical contact crackles with intensity. The seductive power of this image—Cameron, despite all his personal limitations, bending at her feet—recurs twice at the novel's end. Cameron stoops to touch the hem of the medieval gown he chooses as a "parting" gift to Francesca, and when she tells him that she is pregnant, he again kneels before her and kisses the hem of her garment.

The chapters of the novel presented from Cameron's point of view reveal him to be completely aware of his impact on others. He sees the medieval virgin's gown in an advertisement in Francesca's magazine, the same one that features the article on the "new" woman; he tears the ad from the magazine and sets in motion the precise plan that will bring Francesca back into his control. The desire for control is quite clear; more problematic is the essential nature of Cameron's motives.

Yes, he wants Francesca back. Yes, Francesca has not done a very good job of being a "new" woman, even a new Francesca. To be fair though, she has had only one week to bring about her transformation. Is Cameron considering her feelings and needs or his own when he constructs the fiction of the medieval virgin—which he couches in realistic terms, suggesting that she could do him an enormous favor by returning to California and wearing the gorgeous gown, so perfect for her, when he announces his run for attorney general? If she cannot do that, can she at least allow him to buy the gown and hang it in her abandoned closet, a symbol of the inescapable power of his image of her? He knows his power and what effect it has on his wife, but is he right in believing that what he wants is the best option for Francesca?

When Characters Write Their Own "Fictions"

These questions lie at the heart of *Glass People,* and the novel's conclusion, while ambiguous on a realistic level, suggests that both Cameron and Francesca are able to construct more viable lives than the Empsons in *The Perfectionists.* The Bolts' approach is not ideal, despite its overtones of myth and fairy tale, but it is the first step toward the crucial connection in Godwin's work between techniques of fiction and the shaping of real life, as practiced by her characters.

In many ways Cameron and Francesca Bolt are the two dominant strains in the archetypal "Godwin woman" split and forced into direct conflict with each other. Cameron is Godwin's most extreme rendering of the impulse to order and control that creates, finally, the impulse to fiction, either as artist or as artist-of-one's-life, an impulse central to all of Godwin's subsequent protagonists. Francesca is her most extreme example of the contrary impulse to torpor and drift, to a completely passive life. Francesca is equally representative of the fundamental dissatisfaction any Godwin character eventually feels when that impulse to passivity is not resisted.

By separating these impulses, Godwin sacrifices the richer internal conflicts that emerge in the later work when a single character is struggling with the implications of both impulses at every turn in her life. But the aesthetic act of the separation may well have allowed Godwin to clarify and resolve her own struggle with these impulses as an author-narrator and to discover that this essential conflict can provide the source for any number of characters and plots.

In addition, the narrative exploration of Cameron and Francesca as types embodying the philosophical concerns most important to Godwin as a novelist creates a recognition in them that their creator surely must share. Cameron and Francesca learn to create a fiction that allows them each to enjoy compromised, if not ideal, success. Through the magic of these "fictions," they need not torment themselves with the fact of the compromise. The power of fiction making is that one can proceed as if the fiction were truth.

Chapter Three
Suspended Women: *The Odd Woman* and *Violet Clay*

In the epigraph to *The Odd Woman,* Gail Godwin quotes C. G. Jung on the connection between personal (limited) knowledge and universal (infinite) knowledge. Jung says, "In knowing ourselves to be unique in our personal combination—that is, ultimately limited—we possess also the capacity for becoming conscious of the infinite. But only then!"

In this novel and her next, *Violet Clay,* Godwin attains a maturity in both her protagonists and her narrative voice that is missing from the two earlier novels. The growth is, in large measure, the result of a recognition in the characters and the narrators of the important distinction and the inescapable link between self and other that Jung describes.

Jane Clifford, the protagonist of *The Odd Woman,* differs from her predecessors in that she accepts a limited vision of herself and her life without sacrificing the intensity of her struggle to establish uniqueness and independence—in fact, oddness. Through her acceptance of a limited sense of self, she comes to have an enormous capacity for examining others, for *knowing* the context of her life in ways that Dane Empson and Francesca Bolt never could. Ironically, just as Jung suggests, the more aware of her limited self she becomes, the broader and more sympathetic her knowledge of the infiniteness of human experience becomes.

With Violet Clay, the protagonist of the novel that bears her name, Godwin goes a step further, allowing Violet to transform her broader sense of self and other into art, a visible expression of her sense of the universal. It is, however, crucial to the development of that sense within Violet that her journey toward producing art truly begins in a journey to discover the self through immersion in the past, her own and that of her family.

By the time Godwin finishes *Violet Clay,* she has emerged as a mature writer, clear in her personal vision and free of the strain and limitations visible in the first two novels. *The Odd Woman* and *Violet Clay* develop, for the first time, what are among the most important themes in Godwin's fiction. In both, the main character is forced into direct and inescapable confrontation with family. While the treatment of the protagonists' backgrounds in

The Perfectionists and *Glass People* suggests that familial relationships are significant to adult characters, in those novels Godwin does not delve into the complexities of those backgrounds.

In *The Odd Woman* and *Violet Clay* it is impossible for either woman to progress toward her goals until she confronts her past and clarifies in her own mind how that past, both family and legend, has contributed to her sense of self and her ability or inability to pursue the path she has chosen.

A second major theme that emerges in these novels is the importance of work to Godwin's characters. Jane Clifford is a literature teacher, and Violet Clay is a painter. Each is truly absorbed by her profession at the same time that she feels enormous doubt about her ability to realize the ambition born out of that obsession. The struggle to be true to one's work, one's art, is among Godwin's most important subjects, and in Dane Empson and Francesca Bolt she is able to demonstrate only what the lack of significant work means to her characters. In Jane Clifford and Violet Clay, she accomplishes the much harder task of making work integral to the characters' struggles.

The relationship between protagonists and male figures—in the earlier novels, between wives and husbands—becomes less important in these novels. Jane Clifford is involved in an affair with a married man, Gabriel Weeks. Because he is married and lives in another state, they are not as intimately involved in each other's lives as is the case in *The Perfectionists* and *Glass People*, where the Empsons and the Bolts are hard to consider outside the marital relationship. Most of Jane's life is lived separate from Gabriel. He is portrayed as a sometime lover, an angel who drops in for an occasional weekend or who summons Jane, as from on high, to a getaway in a faraway and make-believe world—New York City, for example.

Even more significant is the increased ironic distance of the narrator in regard to the male's power. Both narrator and reader in *The Odd Woman* are aware almost from the outset that Jane is a more powerful person than Gabriel. Thus, the position of the female protagonist is less ambiguous than it was in the earlier works, and much of the reader's (and presumably the author-narrator's) pleasure comes from watching Jane become as aware of her personal power as the reader has been all along. Because Violet is a first-person narrator with her own sense of irony about her personal power, Godwin again moves beyond the earlier protagonists and narrators, who lack irony.

With *Violet Clay*, Godwin goes a step further in lessening the importance of the male-female relationship. The novel opens as a relationship ends for Violet. She finds herself alone in her New York apartment, facing the prospects of supporting herself financially and emotionally. When Francesca Bolt finds herself alone in the city, she lasts a week before Cameron comes and lures her back to the rarefied atmosphere of their California life. Violet has no such figure in her life, and therefore Godwin must, for the first time, develop a protagonist completely outside the context of a sexual relationship.

Whether a natural consequence of the diminished importance of the male-female relationship or a manifestation of the more thorough development of her protagonists, in these novels the women find themselves involved in much richer, much more complex relationships with other women than is possible in the stories of Dane and Francesca. Jane and Violet both find at least partial answers to the questions they pose for themselves in their contact with other women—family members, colleagues, friends, even relative strangers. These relationships all pass beyond the surface quality that marks the contact between women in the earlier books, and in no case is there the strong element of the bizarre or the grotesque that appears in the relationships that Dane and Francesca have with other females.

In short, *The Odd Woman* and *Violet Clay* are fuller and richer stories than *The Perfectionists* and *Glass People*. However, the Godwin female is still a woman who wishes to maintain control over her life, who wants to have an ideal mate, who longs to be her best self with grace and dignity. The differences that emerge to make the later work so much better are, in large measure, the result of more focus in the characters and in the narrators.

Listening to the Stories She Could Tell

The plot of *The Odd Woman* depends on three major events in Jane Clifford's life. First, there is her affair with Gabriel. After two years of tenuous, unquestioning love, Jane feels that she must have some answers. She wants to know where they stand. Gabriel has applied for a Guggenheim fellowship, and when the story opens during Jane's semester break from her university, they both await word of whether he will get the appointment. If he does, they plan to live together in London during the upcoming academic year while he does research on the pre-Raphaelites. If he doesn't, Jane is unsure about what will happen to their relationship.

The security of her position with Gabriel is complicated by the second crucial plot point. Jane's appointment at her university is temporary, mirroring the tentative nature of her romance. Since it is already well into the academic year and she has no career plans for the next, she feels uneasy about her professional future. Even if the Guggenheim comes through for

Gabriel and she spends the year in London with him, she has a hard time imagining just what she will do with herself.

These relatively latent conflicts are brought to the forefront by the major precipitating event of the novel. As the week of her vacation begins, Jane receives word that her grandmother, Edith Dewar Barnstorff, has died. After Jane's mother, Kitty, married Jane's stepfather, Ray Sparks, Edith became the young Jane's role model and safe haven from the oppressive and threatening atmosphere of her violated home with her mother. Even in Jane's adulthood, Edith served as a kind of mental guide and confessor figure for her granddaughter, and as Jane faces the prospect of returning home for her funeral, she cannot escape confrontation with her past, which leads to serious questioning about her present and her future.

The present time of *The Odd Woman* is, then, the week of Jane's vacation. During that week she attends Edith's funeral in the southern city where she grew up, then flies to New York to meet Gabriel. While she is in the South, she confronts the ghost of the family legend, Edith's sister, Cleva, who eloped with but did not marry the villain of a traveling melodrama. Cleva shortly returns in a coffin, accompanied by an illegitimate child. The story of Cleva is the story that has shaped Jane's childhood. Part of Edith's legacy to her, the story hits Jane full in the face as she encounters Frances, Cleva's daughter, at the funeral and as she and Kitty go through Edith's things afterward.

But Cleva's story is at best ambiguous, and as Jane searches for the truth, the final explanation of how Cleva lived and died after leaving the safety of her home, she begins to realize that her own life is just as ambiguous and unclear to her. The idea that women live according to the stories they are told is important to Jane's quest and throughout the body of Godwin's work. Cleva's story is the most melodramatic and the most consciously used (by Edith) to shape an individual woman's life (Jane's), but one of the major motifs of this novel is the connection between story and experience in the lives of women.

The book takes its title from a nineteenth-century novel by George Gissing, *The Odd Women,* which Jane, an insomniac, spends the first night of her vacation trying to read. She will be teaching the novel to her students after the semester break. In the nineteenth-century connotation of *odd,* an odd woman was unmarried. As Godwin shifts the focus from a group, Gissing's story, to the singular story of a specific odd woman, she reflects perhaps the shift toward the personal that is typical of much twentieth-century literature. But *The Odd Woman* is also the story of several odd women, Cleva being one—she never marries even though she has a child.

Edith, too, is a kind of odd woman in that she is a widow long before Jane's birth, so Jane's only sense of her grandmother is of a woman living without a man.

Jane's early years are spent with Edith and Kitty, also a young widow, and Jane's best friend from college, Gerda Mulvaney, whom she visits after her disheartening rendezvouz with Gabriel in New York, is yet another version of the odd woman. Divorced and a radical feminist, Gerda surrounds herself with like-minded women as she edits a feminist newspaper, *Feme Sole*. On her flight from her university town to Chicago, where she will connect with a flight to her hometown, Jane encounters Marsha Pederson, a graduate student in her department and the divorced mother of two sons. Marsha is on her way to meet a lover, a married man she met at a convention of the Modern Language Association. She and Jane wind up sharing a hotel room in Chicago, and Jane, who first met Gabriel at a meeting of the MLA, is forced to compare her story with Marsha's.

On the afternoon before leaving for the funeral, Jane has lunch with her friend and colleague Sonia Marks, and the two of them share the story of Jane's half-sister Emily and Emily's marriage. Sonia Marks has her own story, of course, one that is something of a legend in the university town where she and Jane live. Sonia is one of the first literary renderings of a contemporary sociological myth, the superwoman. She has, as Jane sees her life, gotten away with it all. She has a brilliant career, darling children, and another woman's husband for her blissful second marriage. To make matters even more perfect, Sonia Marks attains such bounty at very little personal cost, at least to Jane's eyes. Not odd by Gissing's nineteenth-century definition nor by the modernized connotations of the word that Godwin's other female characters embody, Sonia Marks is, ironically, the oddest woman in the novel, for she is well mated *and* clearly secure in her sense of herself. She is happy.

One function of Godwin's use of these varied and instructive stories of female lives is to establish Jane as a keen observer. Like Dane Empson and Francesca Bolt in the earlier novels, she often stimulates her considerable intelligence through imaginatively entering into the story of someone else's life. But Jane Clifford is a better "reader" of others' stories than are her predecessors, for she moves beyond observing and judging those she encounters. She makes the additional effort to enter into the perspective of the other, to engage sympathetically with experience not her own.

For example, on finding herself trapped in a motel room with Marsha Pederson, a woman to whom she is not particularly close, Jane, exhausted and grieving, at first imagines Marsha's story—the married lover that she's racing off to meet, the nervousness about the dress she's brought with her, her complaints about the circumstances of her life—to be a tawdry version of her own story. She wants to dismiss Marsha, hold her at arm's length, the way that Dane Empson feels about Polly Heykoop and Penelope in *The Perfectionists* or Francesca Bolt feels about the young female reporter who comes to do a feature on her in *Glass People*.

But Jane forces herself to look beyond appearance and to think past her own initial instinct to dismiss the other woman as somehow beneath her or unworthy of her sympathies. She enters Marsha's point of view, however briefly, to see the other woman's story from a perspective different from her own. Having done this further imagining, Jane sees that Marsha's story might be as noble or more so than her own. After all, Marsha has two young sons, and part of her quest is to find a father for those boys. Is that not a worthier goal than Jane's own pursuit of a married man for no reason greater than her own personal satisfaction?

The point here is not that Jane Clifford decides that Marsha Pederson is a "better" person than she. She does not. There is, in fact, a somewhat ironic tone even in her sympathetic musings from Marsha's perspective. Nor is the point that she is examining Marsha's story in hopes of finding answers or alternatives for her own life. She is not, really, except as a sort of mental gymnastics that keeps her alert to the possibilities of experience. The point is that the kind of woman Godwin has moved to focus on by the time she writes *The Odd Woman* is a woman better suited to the broad purposes of fiction than are Godwin's earlier heroines.

Thus, because Jane Clifford's thought process is closer to the thought process necessary to developing substantial fiction, Godwin's narrative ability is greatly enhanced. Because the novel is written from Jane's limited point of view, it is especially important that her perspective be an expansive and sympathetic one, if the novel is to fulfill the promise of its epigraph and demonstrate the connection between the personal and the infinite.

Marsha Pederson is not the only character Godwin uses to establish Jane's ability to engage sympathetically with perspectives other than her own. Part of Jane's growth during the novel comes from her using the same imaginative thought process in regard to her mother, her grandmother, Cleva, her sister, Gabriel's wife, Gerda, even the total strangers she encounters on the night she spends in Gerda's apartment after leaving Gabriel in New York. In a sense, her exploration of these stories is an approach, however inadequate for its limitations, toward the infinite nature of the female experience. Jane Clifford is about the business of understanding what it is to be a woman, not only for herself but in a larger sense as well.

This is, of course, fairly common territory in contemporary women's fiction, but Godwin does not leave it at this. Jane Clifford's true goal, her most important quest, is for what she calls "her best life."[1] Early in the novel, Godwin presents this goal in less concrete terms. She says of Jane: "she wanted to understand this life. . . . What she wanted was a metaphor of her own" (*OW*, 3). By the time that Kitty drives Jane to the airport after the funeral and after they have spent an afternoon going through Edith's things and drinking sherry together, Jane can say to her mother the specific thing she wants—*her* best life.

The connection between seeking one's best life through understanding that life, finding one's personal metaphor, and the motif of hearing and reading stories, even creating them, as the means to that end is clear in the novel. Jane Clifford insists on an integrity in that process that marks her as the first of what will be the definitive Godwin heroine. That integrity can be defined by Jane's personal attitude toward stories themselves.

Early in the novel she thinks about the role of stories in human lives and realizes the appeal and the danger of living according to story: "Stories were all right, as long as you read them as what they were: single visions, one person's way of interpreting something. You could learn from stories, be warned by stories. But stories, by their very nature, were Procrustean. Even the longest of them had to end somewhere. If a living human being tried to squeeze himself into a particular story, he might find vital parts of himself lopped off. Even worse, he might find himself unable to get out again!" (*OW*, 43).

Women in particular, it seems in Godwin's world, are subject to the lure of story in that they internalize the stories they have been told and then measure their lives against those artificial renderings of experience. Whether the stories are falsely ideal, as is the case with many fairy tales or with an outsider's view of the life of someone such as Sonia Marks, or false in the intimidating nature of their bleak melodrama, as is the case with the tale of Cleva that shapes Jane's early years, they set up barriers that are extremely difficult for an individual woman to hurdle as she moves toward shaping a life for herself.

Jane Clifford's attitude toward stories as containers that might require a person to lop off vital parts of himself or herself or as traps from which a person might never escape connects her to Cameron Bolt, a character who also sees life as a matter of shapes and containers. But Cameron wants to find ways to make experience fit into the containers (stories) he finds appropriate. Jane wants to be sure that the shape (story) she settles on is her own and involves no limitations on or omissions of what is vital to her.

In her novels Godwin does not create a protagonist who is a writer of stories until her seventh, *A Southern Family,* but Jane Clifford is the first step in Godwin's evolving definition of the best life. To live the best life, one must not only absorb stories; she must also interpret or create them. Thus, Jane is a teacher of stories, one whose life is based on words. She also strives to know and understand precisely the words and stories that touch her life and to exert some control over those forces.

Godwin's next protagonist, Violet Clay, is an artist, someone who creates stories in pictures rather than words. Cate, one of the main characters in *A Mother and Two Daughters,* is a teacher of drama, among other subjects, so that the interpreting of stories takes on another dimension and comes closer to reality. Justin Stokes, the main character in *The Finishing School,* grows up to become an actress after having Ursula DeVane, a consummate actress, as her mentor. Finally, in *A Southern Family* there is Clare, who is a successful novelist, challenged by her half-brother to write a story that she cannot tie up neatly, a story that defies, to use Jane Clifford's language, the inherent Procrustean nature of stories.

If Jane's life is examined in terms of the stories that shape it, her progress through the novel is a journey to understand and move beyond the story of Cleva and her disaster, which signifies the larger need to understand the story of family and past. Her journey also involves coming to terms with and leaving behind the story of her affair with Gabriel, a story that she creates and largely controls. Finally, both of these major influences on Jane's life are too limiting. They are obstacles to her primary goal of living her best life and must be revised, rewritten, to put them in their proper, their lesser, place.

Edith's death leaves a large gap in the foundation of Jane's sense of herself. She is very much the product of Edith's perspective. As she faces the prospect of entering the world of family again, Jane vows not to revert to the role she usually plays. She will not allow their image of her to be her.

As her plane descends into their territory, she thinks: "They had stood so for years of her landings, these people, waiting for her to come back to them, expecting her to come back, never doubting she had any choice but to fall back from the sky into their nets of family and region and social standing and—most compelling weave of all—their image of her, Jane, their Jane" (*OW,* 83). Despite her vow, the moment the plane lands and she approaches them, she bursts into tears and wants only to be their Jane, to have them tend and control her in just the way she has promised herself they will not.

It is not that Jane does not love her family. For Edith and Kitty, her love is profound and inescapable. She is also fond of her half-sister and her two half-brothers. Her only reservations are about Ray Sparks, the stepfather to whom Kitty has been married for 25 years. The problem is that Jane does not want to accept their version of her life, but it is so safe, so easy to fall into, that she realizes she must live away from them and the world they represent in order to grow beyond that version of herself.

When she leaves the family to join Gabriel in New York, Jane spends part of her time researching the melodrama that changed Cleva's life and, thus, that shaped Jane's own sense of the world from her earliest memories. She discovers that the actor who played the villain in that play and in the lives of her family for all those years was probably not the villain at all in Cleva's life. The "real" villain was just as likely the "hero" of the melodrama. The awful ambiguity produced by her research, her visit to the actor, and a subsequent reexamination of the faded program on which Cleva scrawls her final message to the family convinces Jane that the truth about oneself and others is much more complex and organic than the lessons of her childhood would have allowed.

In Search of Villains and Angels

Armed with new insight about her past, Jane has the courage to reevaluate her present situation with Gabriel. She decides to leave him rather than to wait out the decision about the fellowship, their year in London, the chance of a future together. As in both of Godwin's earlier novels, the conflict between the protagonist and her husband or lover is central to this novel. The major difference in Jane Clifford is that her role in the male-female relationship is more active and aware than that of either Dane Empson or Francesca Bolt. With John Empson and Cameron Bolt, these women find themselves carried off by a force beyond their control or understanding.

Although Jane shares some of her predecessors' tendencies to give the self over to the male force in their lives and although Gabriel, by virtue of both his marriage and his nature, is in some ways beyond her control, Jane is also entirely conscious of her role in creating and shaping their relationship. Unlike Dane or Francesca, Jane understands that power, its capacities and its limitations.

Gabriel Weeks first comes to Jane's attention when she attends a session at the Modern Language Association convention. From that encounter, without any actual contact at all, she carries an image of Gabriel as a hero, a talisman for the completion of her dissertation. In the session, he comes across, for Jane, as a man of courageous vision, dedicated to his work, his personal vision of the world, standing alone against the forces of fashionable cynicism represented by the scholar who challenges Gabriel during the program, a professor named Zimmer. Throughout the novel, Jane thinks of "Zimmer voices" as "voices making light of things they really care about, belittling great ideas, reducing to ironic trills and singsongs their profoundest hopes and fears" (*OW*, 214), and she sees Gabriel as the great preserver of integrity and value, refusing to follow fashion down the essentially destructive route of cynical, ironic disavowal.

The tendency toward cynicism is something that Jane herself must guard against, and in that sense Gabriel serves a different function for her than the earlier males do for their women. John and Cameron are largely responsible for defining Dane and Francesca. Jane, much more sure of who and what she is, sees in Gabriel a model for a specific quality that she has already recognized as a weakness in herself. Her concern about that shortcoming is not merely personal. It is related to her sense of her work and ultimately to her vision of life. She thinks of it this way:

Being an articulate denigrator, instructing in a cynical singsong, was easy. . . . The risk was to be a visionary and utter phrases of unfashionable hope. Patterns of alienation, despair, disgust, denial, disintegration, and derangement lay on her desk at school as thick and plentiful as Ray's sale towels: anthologies that poured in by the dozen, gifts from publishers concerned with being relevant. No, what was needed were a few more lonely patterns of desire. (*OW*, 118)

Impressed by Gabriel at the session, she searches out his monograph in the library when she gets back home. Published more than 20 years earlier, it is a scholarly treatise that attempts to classify love as characterized by three pre-Raphaelite painters. The idea of classifying and categorizing love is appealing to Jane, who writes to Gabriel, receives a formal, disappointing response, and loses her quietly unfolding vision of hope. But he follows the initial response with love-painting postcards and a bouquet of spring flowers, and she eventually goes to St. Louis to meet "this man whose acquaintance she had made almost totally through her own devisings and dreamings" (*OW*, 222).

Thus, from the outset, she realizes that Gabriel is, in a sense, a story that she tells herself in order to fill a vacuum in her life. He is an effort to reaffirm what she wants to believe is true. In talking to Kitty, Jane explains what it is that she hopes to learn about love:

But I want to know . . . whether there is eternal love between a man and a woman. I want to know whether there has ever existed in this world a lasting, lively love in which a man and a woman exist, for years and years and years, taking sustenance and delight from this love, being able to do things better *because* of this love rather than in spite of it. I want to settle this question of whether we need our other half, or if that's just some old story born out of economic necessities. (*OW,* 166)

The dissertation Jane writes as she devises and dreams her relationship with Gabriel into existence is entitled *The Theme of Guilt in the Novels of George Eliot,* and part of Jane's inspiration to seek the kind of love she describes to her mother comes from her sense of Eliot's relationship with her lover, also a married man. In a letter to a friend Eliot describes her love as energizing, the happiness that comes from being together making everything easy. To Kitty, Jane says, "I want that kind of love which brings such energies" (*OW,* 168). Gabriel, with his ready scheme of love, is to be her test of whether she can have what she wants, of whether what she wants really exists.

When Jane decides to leave Gabriel in New York, to give up on her fragile hope that the love she desires does exist and is available to her, the question is resolved not only for her but also it would appear for Godwin. In the novels that follow *The Odd Woman* the questions about love that Jane seeks to answer are not asked by the protagonists. There is a suggestion in Clare's relationship with her lover in *A Southern Family* that such a relationship can exist and also perhaps in the more tentative relationships attained by Cate and Lydia in *A Mother and Two Daughters,* but the pursuits of all these women are different. The relationships they achieve are background, just part of the context of their lives and certainly without the lofty trappings in which Jane tries to dress her liaison with Gabriel.

She leaves Gabriel not because he does not love her and not because they cannot continue to have the relationship they have had for almost two years. She realizes that he will allow her to love him and will go on loving her for as long as she will let him. She leaves him because she comes to recognize that the thing she wants from him is finally a denial of herself, a way to avoid what she really is and what she really wants.

She tells him that she wants him to help her "stop wanting things so badly. . . . I want you to tell me how to be detached, as you are. . . . Please, teach me how to take things or leave them, to take *people* or leave them" (*OW,* 250). It is an essential characteristic of Jane Clifford and of all Godwin's subsequent protagonists that, although there is a strong temptation to stop *wanting,* to be able to take or leave people, experiences, the stuff of life itself, one must not succumb. For it is in that sort of surrender and compromise that one becomes ordinary, unexceptional, loses one's chance to transcend the mundane and to know what lies beyond. The perpetual struggle to keep wanting, to take rather than leave, is frightening, tiring, disillusioning, unending, but it is the only thing, finally, that makes life bearable for the Godwin characters that both readers and narrators care most about.

Those characters are not the ones who stop wanting or who leave parts of their experience by the wayside. They are not the ones who are like Gabriel and learn his lessons. Jane recognizes this truth early in the novel, thinking of her life in terms of story once again. On the morning of Edith's death, she sees herself this way: "she had not written herself into any premature endings. False middles, perhaps, but there was time, she felt, still time, still hope to do, be anything, *as long as every experience,* every incident, pleasant and unpleasant, trivial and annoying, *could be used in some way toward the spiritual financing of her quest* [emphasis added]" (*OW,* 44).

Jane leaves Gabriel because she realizes that what she wants from him will ultimately hinder rather than aid in her quest for her best life. This recognition is crucial to all of Godwin's subsequent protagonists. It serves as the basis for each woman's pursuit of that same goal, her best life. When Jane reaches her crisis in her relationship with Gabriel, she cries. At first the crying has a defeated quality: "Truly exhausted, she felt she had come to the end of something. She did not want to think or try anymore. She only wanted to be allowed to go on crying until she had cried herself away" (*OW,* 277).

Almost immediately, however, the crying takes on another quality, one much truer to Jane's character and to the character that typifies the Godwin woman:

She started to cry again. But now her crying was not a flushing out, from exhaustion and resignation, of all the impurities of the day, all the tiring, troublesome strainings of her ego; this new fit of weeping engorged her, soaked the old ego into her again, making her turgid and defensively alert. She was back on her guard, and for your guard you needed your ego. What so competent as the ego to assess the strategic losses and negotiate back lost points? (*OW,* 279)

It is through the continual assertion of ego that one escapes the dangers of stories—of having to lop off essential parts of the self, of being trapped within an unsuitable story. The ego helps one be indestructible in that it allows one to preserve the self. Gabriel helps Jane toward this recognition, which means he helps her toward her real goal rather than toward the false, lesser goal that she says she wants him to lead her to.

This concept of indestructibility is explored in some detail by Godwin:

> Her lover had called her indestructible. She had a glimmer of what he meant. You remained indestructible by eluding for dear life the hundreds and thousands of already written, already completed stories. You climbed out of them before they rose too high. You reminded yourself that you were more than they were, that you had to write yourself as you went along, that your story could not and should not possibly be completed until *you* were: *i.e.,* dead. Even then, no matter how good it was, others might learn from it, be strengthened or even transformed by it, but it could never, never be a perfect fit for anyone else again. (*OW*, 44)

To be indestructible, therefore, one must be odd, must have a story that is one's own rather than a retooled version of an existing story.

Shopping for the Best Self

In a scene that is quite extended, given its location late in the novel and its relative unimportance to the literal plot, Jane enters Saks in New York to buy something that will make her more attractive. She is there partly to kill time while Gabriel goes about his business and partly because of the stinging words of the cab driver who brings her from the airport. He suggests that she could be a pretty woman if she would fix herself up a little.

Going shopping recalls for her the shopping trips of her childhood and adolescence when Edith would call ahead to the department store to announce their arrival, when Mr. Blum, the owner, would wait to escort them into the proper department, and when, magically, "ordinary clothes" could be turned into "Jane's own clothes." Alone and grown up in Saks, she is dismayed by the "hundreds and hundreds of clothes . . . crammed waiting for the right woman to come along and transform them, slip her proud flesh into their emptiness so they could fulfill themselves" (*OW*, 310).

The important difference in the shopping trips with Edith and the one she makes alone in New York is the way that Jane sees her own role in each case. In the earlier trip, the clothes were magically transformed for her, especially to suit her. In the later episode, she feels enormous pressure to transform the clothes, to bring her own secure identity to them and give them life. In addition to the increased responsibility and pressure she feels in Saks, there is the awareness that the number of choices available to her is limited by the choices and experiences that precede her current trip. (In an interview after the publication of *A Mother and Two Daughters,* Godwin told a reporter that shopping was a terrifying experience for her, in much the way it is for Jane Clifford [Vespa, 70].)

The decisions, the choices, of the past are irrevocable, and Jane sees that most people choose one of two alternatives: they "curse and continue to fight the irrevocable, pretend it hadn't happened yet," or they "find soft, tactful retreats, dimmed to the specifications of one's diminishing hopes" (*OW,* 313). But Jane wants a different alternative. She wants to know what lies one step beyond the irrevocable: "That one step further was what interested her" (*OW,* 314).

Having made the decision to be alone, to remain odd, Jane returns to her midwestern apartment in the university town to face what lies one more step beyond. At the beginning of the novel, before she faces Edith's death or the break with Gabriel, she describes to Sonia Marks, a woman who has never lived alone, what being on her own feels like:

These awful states of dangerous awareness, as if someone had slit a gash in that thin web of sanity that holds in my wholeness, and I start to believe that this web is the only thing that makes me *me.* Inside the web is a sort of liquid state, which contains all the things in everybody, all the things in the world, not "mine" anymore than anybody else's. And I am terrified that this liquid will start running out of me and seek its natural source, some kind of Source Sea which contains elements of everybody, all kinds of habits and attitudes and characteristics of future people. If this should happen, I know I will cease to be. What was "I" will be a crumpled empty skin, a web vacated. (*OW,* 63)

When she returns to her apartment, then, she knows that she is taking a risk. The self she seeks to preserve and the integrity she chooses to maintain in her life are always at risk because they are protected only by the thin web of her sanity, and that sanity is forever challenged by the dangerous and powerful pull of otherness. Her choice is *not* to be totally removed from others, for they provide the experience with which she will continue to finance her quest. It is, rather, to prevent herself from being absorbed by the omnipresent Source Sea.

The Odd Woman's closing image suggests that art is the best defense against the confusion of the Source Sea. When Jane gets back to her apartment, Sonia Marks calls to say that it is likely that Jane can teach another year at the university, which means that she will at least be able to support herself. Then Portia Prentiss calls. Portia is a young black woman who should have failed Jane's class, but Jane gives her a *C.* Now Portia is calling to tell her that she has enrolled in Jane's class for the next semester, having flunked all her other courses.

Confronted so immediately with the realities of her life, Jane recognizes that even so dramatic a crisis as she has passed through in the preceding week does not change the basic structures of existence. Life goes on. Thinking of Portia and of Edith and Kitty and Gabriel and of all her past, she thinks as she talks to the young woman, "I should have known. I am not going to be allowed to get away with anything in this life. I shall have to live with the consequences of every action" (*OW,* 417).

As she faces this awesome truth, this overwhelming responsibility, she hears music coming from a little concrete house behind her apartment. The sound soothes and comforts her: "Her heartbeat slowed from melodramatic terror to its usual insomniac tick." Calmer, she can see the hope in the effort of the "soul at the piano," a human being as limited as herself, "trying to organize the loneliness and the weather and the long night into something of abiding shape and beauty" (*OW,* 419).

Is Work Better than Sex?

This conclusion, small and fragile in its hopefulness, is explored more fully in *Violet Clay.* The search for the ideal mate is abandoned, it seems, when Jane Clifford abandons Gabriel Weeks in New York. Sex itself becomes much more realistic in that Godwin's protagonists after Jane Clifford do not look for an imagined ideal fusion with a mate, an absorption of self. Jane realizes in her final sexual episode with Gabriel that she has not, even in their best moment, completely abandoned herself to her lover.

She has, however, experienced such a state of fusion in her work. When she is in the library finishing her dissertation and creating the mental image of Gabriel that leads to their affair, she finds herself transformed: "Here she was pure and light, stripped of her usual fears about her own inadequacies, about the uncertainty of the future. . . . For the first time in her life, she was where she wanted to be; she was at one with her task. She *was* her work" (*OW,* 214).

The development of Violet Clay as a protagonist is an extension of these qualities and recognitions in Jane Clifford. Without a man when the novel begins, Violet must explore herself through an effort to reengage with her work, painting. She must try to organize the mess of her life and of her family's past into something of abiding shape and beauty. Her eventual success takes the form of a painting that she calls *Suspended Woman,* a visual rendering of the feeling Jane Clifford experiences in those heady moments within her isolated library carrel.

The idea of woman suspended between worlds or options, as represented by Violet's first important work of art, is a major turning point in Godwin's fiction. In her first two novels, Godwin is concerned with protagonists desperate to feel secure and fixed in a world that is familiar without being confining. In *The Odd Woman,* with Jane Clifford, Godwin moves toward a woman who can accept the ambiguous and organic nature of her reality and who can resist the urge to falsify that reality with an artificial security. What Violet Clay strives to capture in her painting of her neighbor, Sam, is what Godwin has been working toward as well: "The painting's challenge would be how well I could capture that state of *precariousness,* how well I could evoke, through paint, choices hanging in the balance, the way different thicknesses (like different individuals) strove to impose their color against all that would go on anyway."[2]

In *The Perfectionists* and *Glass People,* the male characters, John Empson and Cameron Bolt, occupy much of the narrative and are, in many ways, as interesting to narrator and reader as the female protagonists. These men share uncommonly high expectations of others, particularly their wives, and often find themselves angry and disappointed when those expectations are not met. Their wives, on the other hand, share the frustration of an unfulfilled, undefined self. This split along sexual lines diffuses some of the focus and power of the novels' plots, but, in Jane Clifford, Godwin fuses these qualities, strengthening the narration and the insight into character. Jane herself comprehends her dual nature when she thinks about her discontent: "And beyond the problem of her frustrated expectations of others was the ever-present problem of her unclear, undefined, unresolved self" (*OW,* 21).

Fusion of important thematic and character motifs within one person goes a step further in the portrait of Sam, Violet Clay's enigmatic neighbor and the model for her breakthrough painting. Whereas Jane Clifford embodies the key character traits of unrealistic expectations of others and ill-defined self, Samantha De Vere is another sort of hybrid, also of two important Godwin strains. Violet says of Sam, "She was like some hybrid woman, a composite of what had always been and what could be" (*VC,* 305).

This important ability to hold the past and the possibilities for the future within oneself is crucial to the evolving sense of what it takes to be a successful woman in Godwin's world. The symbolic visual rendering of that woman in the portrait of Sam is reinforced by the way that Violet's own sense of time changes as a result of her experiences during the novel. As she is working on the painting that will change her life, Violet contemplates her altered view of time:

> For years of my life I developed my negative propensity for time travel. At a moment's notice I could plunge into some awful moment of the past (or some awfuler fantasy about the future) and come back with enough material to take a lugubrious bath in. Now I am becoming adept in making the positive trip as well. I send my mental spaceship to points past or future and it frequently comes back with old buds of present blossomings . . . or sometimes a bold design for fruits to come. (*VC*, 306)

The epigraph to *Violet Clay* (from Emanuel Schikaneder's libretto for *The Magic Flute*) asks the question "When will my eyes find the light?" and answers it, ambiguously, "Soon, soon, Youth, or never." Violet Clay, who is the same age as Jane Clifford, 32, on the brink of middle-age, finds her light just in time, as Jane Clifford hears the musical equivalent of that light just in time to land them each firmly on the side of the unending quest for abiding shape and beauty. Godwin's subsequent work will make characters who share in their decision its central concern. It will be about characters, primarily women, who learn to live in suspension and to draw power from that state.

The opening sentence of *Violet Clay* signals a shift in Godwin's approach to fiction. It is her first novel written in first person. That sentence is short, simple, declarative: "I am a painter" (*VC*, 3). The reader immediately notices the straightforward assertion of this character's identity. Then her present sense of herself as a painter is contrasted with a past identity, a point in her life when she was doing "hack" work. This clear sense of self, both now and as one existed in the past, signals a different kind of woman than the protagonists who preceded her. Violet is a woman who knows what she is and where she came from. Because of the first-person narrative and the shift in time from present to past, the reader is aware from the beginning that Violet has undergone dramatic growth in character. The novel is her version of how that growth occurs.

As in *The Odd Woman*, the precipitating event in *Violet Clay* is the death of a relative who has played a major role in shaping the character of the novel's protagonist. Violet has lost her lover and her job as an illustrator of covers for gothic romance novels when she receives word that her Uncle Ambrose has committed suicide at his cabin in the Adirondacks.

Ambrose, author years earlier of *Looking for the Lora Lee*, a successful novel based on the life of Violet's mother, has retreated to the cabin to try to complete a second book. His suicide, coming as it does on the heels of Violet's own collapsed love affair and job, forces her to question her own art and her devotion to it. It is through that examination that she is able to attain a valuable new perspective by the novel's end. The experience also allows her to create art true to her vision of herself and her craft, to fulfill the promise she made to herself when she left her marriage and came to New York to be an artist nine years earlier.

As Edith Wharton's heroine Lily Bart (whose story is central to Jane Clifford's decision making in New York) fears being consumed by dinginess, Godwin's protagonists, including Violet, fear ordinariness. When she comes to the city at 23 to be an artist, part of what Violet flees is the ordinary story in which she finds herself trapped.

Child of an ill-fated marriage between Milledge Clay, the father she never knows because he is killed in World War II, and Liza Lee Clay, the mother who commits suicide out of grief, Violet begins life by adopting The Orphan's story as her own. But The Orphan is obliged to feel gratitude for anything that comes her way, a trait at odds with Violet's "sharp fault-finding ego" (VC, 10). Her paternal grandmother, Georgette Clay, rears Violet on the East Battery of Charleston, South Carolina, where they live in genteel poverty, selling off pieces of their heritage in the form of antiques to finance the appearance of their lives.

The story of Georgette's marriage to Charles Clay serves as a warning to Violet. Georgette dreamed of a career as an accomplished pianist, but she abandons those dreams on the brink of a Carnegie Hall audition in order to be a proper wife and mother. Unfortunately, Violet does not heed the warning and allows herself to be absorbed by still another cliche plot. In the summer after she graduates from college, Violet comes to live in the Clay house to begin a career as a serious painter, but destiny intervenes in the person of Lewis Lanier, cousin of Violet's godmother, Violet Pardee, whom her namesake refers to as Big V.

The painting that Violet is working on when she meets Lewis is called *Wasteful Sea,* in part a reference to the sea that takes her young mother's life. But the title also echoes Jane Clifford's image of the Source Sea that can rush out and engulf the person who is not careful to preserve the integrity provided by the fragile web of self. By abandoning *Wasteful Sea* to marry Lewis, Violet imagines that she was fulfilling a desire to be "dragged screaming" to her destiny (VC, 11), an image borrowed from the language of the romance novels she illustrates.

Unfortunately, having arrived, she finds her destiny unsatisfactorily confining and must face the terrifying prospect that the desirable destiny may prove further and further away, year after year. Marriage to Lewis—a perfectly ordinary young attorney who wants family, children, the whole familiar story that Violet flees into when she chooses him—alerts her to the dangers of comfort and familiarity for the artist: "But I had gone all funny and languorous. There was something delicious and sensual about my abdication. I had walked willingly into the trap of those tough and cunning old friends [her grandmother and Big V], playing us off like their pet summer puppets" (*VC,* 31). She goes on to describe the direct impact on her work: "I didn't touch a paintbrush those first months of captivity. What for? The colors of satisfaction oozed out of my very pores. . . . I lapsed, I gave myself up to my senses, to Womanhood. Lewis was the agent of it, therefore I assumed I loved him" (*VC,* 32).

In these early days of her marriage, Violet comes dangerously close to the kind of paralyzing security and sensual comfort that Francesca Bolt rebels against. But Violet Clay has a much stronger ego than Francesca does. Just as Jane Clifford finds herself weeping about her decision to leave Gabriel in a way that soaks her in the old assertive ego again, Violet Clay finds her hopes for her marriage "had fallen like petals round the indestructible base of her ego" (*VC,* 39). So she leaves Lewis and heads for New York, the scene of Francesca's failed attempt to preserve an independent self, in order to preserve and nurture her ego.

As she makes this move toward affirming the self, she describes her position as having "One foot in the door of the Unknown, the other still holding open its place in the Book of Old Plots" (*VC,* 45). For nine years she clings to a specific Old Plot, holds on to "the wizening image of herself as perpetual maiden as long as she can, perpetually eligible for infinite rescues, infinite salvations, infinite new starts" (*VC,* 14). The cold realities of losing lover, job, and only surviving relative in one fell swoop bring home to Violet the falsity of this plot and send her to her uncle's Plommet Falls cabin to face once and for all the mythic self that she has imagined she can be: Woman Artist.

The paradox of the Woman Artist and love in her life suggests that Violet must sacrifice art to pursue love, as she does when she marries Lewis, and that she must sacrifice love in order to pursue her art, the situation when she leaves her marriage for New York. That situation is mirrored when she realizes, going back to the apartment she has shared with Jake, her departed lover, on the afternoon she is fired by Harrow House, that the room that they have used as a bedroom should have been her studio, the sanctuary of art rather than love. Then, when she leaves that lovers' retreat for Plommet

Falls, once again to seek the true sanctum of Art, she is also again abandoning love, at least temporarily.

Given convention and conditioning, the question Violet faces each time she sets off to be Artist instead of Woman is essentially the same as that faced by Jane Clifford. Is the price of being *not* ordinary being odd? In both of these novels, the answer is apparently yes, but Violet, like Jane, is not ready, at 32, to settle for ordinary. Asking herself, "What if Violet Clay wasn't to be one of the shining ones after all?" she cannot face that possibility. Instead, she chooses to risk oddness: "But: no. I hadn't yet reached that point of resignation where I surrendered the image of my greatest self. If and when that day came, I might as well be dead" (*VC,* 4).

The effort required to serve art and to maintain individual integrity is juxtaposed against not only sexual love but also the biology of femaleness in Violet's story. When she ponders her unhappiness in her marriage and contemplates her options, one of them is pregnancy, the logical next chapter in the Old Plot. When she leaves Lewis she is not pregnant, a reaffirmation that she will not be trapped in that cliche of Womanhood, no matter how seductive its lure. After a discouraging round of gallery calls, however, she toys with the notion of an unexpected pregnancy, leading to a reunion and a retreat into the Old Plot.

Because of her ambivalence about her goal at this point in her life, Violet's initial attempt to seize her destiny as Woman Artist, characterized by her short-lived naivete, results in a biological deus ex machina. After the disappointing reaction to her portfolio, the work of an accomplished student rather than a professional artist, Violet, filled with a sense of failure and rejection, has to suffer the humiliation of sacrificing art to womanhood in the most literal way. Having begun her menstrual period, she must duck into an entryway and use one of her lithographs to cope with the betrayal by her body. Doing so leaves her "Feeling as though I'd come to the end of some good and simple part of my life" (*VC,* 44).

This is indeed a turning point into the compromise and cynicism that dominate the nine years between Violet's first coming to New York and the present time of the novel, the weeks just after Ambrose's suicide. The metaphor for that period is Violet's work as a cover illustrator for the Harrow House gothic romances, work that makes Violet feel as though she is "spending [her] skills on other people's visions" (*VC,* 5), when the goal of the true artist is to bring to fruition a personal vision. This prostituting of skill and vision is mirrored in Ambrose Clay's career after the success of his first novel. Writing under a pseudonym, Ambrose, unable to complete a second "serious literary" work, cranks out travel articles and other records of a frivolous life in order to support himself. Like Violet, he cannot admit to himself or others the true nature of his failure or his feelings about it.

Resisting the Pull of Romance

The metaphor of the romance, especially gothic romance, plays itself out in several important ways in *Violet Clay,* beginning, chronologically, with the melodrama of Violet's parents' story and Ambrose's subsequent rendering of that tale in fiction.

Then there are the stories of Violet's and Ambrose's lovers, each with its twist of the grotesque. For Violet, these include a handicapped publisher of military fiction, a hairdresser who requires her to take complete responsibility for his arousal, a Hungarian artist who will not allow Violet to see him asleep, and Jake, who is sometimes physically abusive. Ambrose's lovers include a *Vogue* editor who has a complete breakdown when he marries someone else and Violet's Mexican roommate from boarding school, a woman young enough to be his daughter, the wife of a diplomat, about whom Ambrose seems to have had a foot fetish.

The detailed nature of the information about these characters and their sexuality is another way in which *Violet Clay* differs from Godwin's earlier work. In both *The Perfectionists* and *Glass People,* the characters have sex and sexual fantasies, but their fantasies have a cool, abstract quality about them, and these early characters tend to mythify sex in a way that Violet has moved beyond (although her uncle probably hasn't and, hence, at least in part, his inability to face the world that Violet decides to embrace). Jane Clifford sees her illicit relationship with Gabriel as a kind of stately dance and never feels the rigid barriers between the two of them dissolve as she longs for them to do. Jane does spend an evening alone in her apartment making pornographic drawings to illustrate the bad novel of a university colleague, but she is drunk when she does and feels so shocked and revolted by what she has created that she clogs her plumbing trying to flush the fruits of her labor down the toilet.

There are, of course, the novels that Violet reads in order to illustrate their covers, particularly those of her friend Milo, who writes under the pen name Arabella Stone. After learning of Ambrose's suicide, Violet goes to Milo's house and spends the night before leaving for Plommet Falls. During that evening and another when she stays with him after giving up her apartment when she decides to move into Ambrose's mountain cabin, Milo shares with Violet the plot of the novel he wants to work on but is having trouble with. He also reveals to her a recurring dream, and out of their discussion the troublesome novel is transformed into what Milo feels will be his most significant work.

Milo is a different kind of character for Godwin, and his relationship with her protagonist is also different, more sustaining and richer than the relationships between friends, male or female, and the protagonists of the earlier novels. In fact, he becomes a surrogate family of sorts for the orphaned Violet, his home providing a haven in which she can begin to move out of the cynicism and compromise she fell into on the day she used her lithograph as a sanitary napkin. The sense of regained innocence, of a second chance, is emphasized by the words Violet uses to describe herself while she is with Milo: "safe," "schoolgirlish," "chastely" (*VC*, 106), and by the feeling that her night in his guest room engenders: "I felt I'd shed all the disillusioned years leading up to tonight" (*VC*, 106).

That Violet can feel so secure and known with Milo indicates her ability to see him as an individual rather than as a stereotype, a character in an Old Plot. When she first meets him, she expects him to be a woman, Arabella Stone, and she expects Arabella to fit her preconceived notion of a romance writer. His being male forces her to drop her preconceptions, and as they work together, talk about being artists, and become friends, Violet comes to rely on Milo in ways that are richer and more rewarding than any relationship portrayed in Godwin's earlier work.

In broadening Violet's level of sympathy and engagement through her relationship with Milo, it is almost as if Godwin is preparing her for what she must face in Plommet Falls. In addition to the necessity of coming to terms with her uncle's suicide, her time in the mountain cabin will also force Violet to face, once and for all, the responsibilities of her talent and her art. In addition, she must deal with her landlady, Minerva Means, sort of a comic nightmare of what Violet might become if she clings too long to the old image of herself as "perpetual maiden." Minerva's gothic mansion, her childish hair ribbons, and her unresolved feelings about her family, especially her sister, make her another warning to Violet.

Violet must also come to understand Sam and her daughter, Cheyenne, who discovered Ambrose's body. Sam's past includes an abusive stepfather who tried to convince her that she was crazy and who lied to her, saying that she had been having sex with him for years, when she had not. When she flees, she is raped by three all-American college students who give her a ride. Cheyenne is the result of the rape, and Sam has become a veritable myth of the self-sufficient woman: good mother, good provider, alive and functioning productively without a man, but, finally, not so embittered that she rules out the idea of future relationships with men—when she is ready.

When Violet first arrives in New York, Ambrose points out to her Ambrose Channel, which lets ships into the city. The channel that shares her uncle's name serves as a metaphor for the path Violet must take to reach her goal. She must pass through Ambrose, who is the embodiment of her past, her family, and her history and of her own potential weaknesses as an artist, in order to reach the place where dream (the idea of being a writer, in Ambrose's case) and reality (actually writing) can, do, and must coexist. By living in Ambrose's last home, by passing imaginatively through his experience, Violet gains the understanding and perspective that allow her to become a true Artist.

If Ambrose, through his suicide, leads Violet to Plommet Falls and provides her with the perspective she needs to paint the pictures she wants to paint, Sam, who lies naked before her and unselfconsciously reveals the story of her life as Violet paints, provides her with a sense of proportion that will carry her through her low points in the future. Violet is well aware of the contributions these two people make to her success. She thinks, "Sam put me into proportion, as Ambrose put me into perspective" (*VC,* 315). Her lifelong role as "Poor Little Me" falls away when she reflects on the stories of these people; Ambrose's surrender, his abandoning his dream of art, and Sam's suffering, so much more vivid and awful than Violet's, draw Violet out of the self and, ironically, make her able to preserve it through the transforming power of art.

Before Ambrose's suicide Violet depends on external motivation to move her toward her goal: "all those dusks and dawns ago, waiting for it to happen, waiting for my fate to begin shaping itself. I waited mostly for the phone to ring, for Ambrose to call and ask me out again, for the lady from *Vogue* to call and offer me a job, for some outside voice to explain to me what I was doing there and where I was to go next" (*VC,* 107).

But her experience in the mountains leads her to recognition of her responsibility for her own dream:

There I had crouched in the shadows of my own potential. I had my feelings and I had my materials, but I didn't know how to make one work for the other. There I sat, waiting for something to happen, for the phone to ring, for help to come from outside. That something was happening inside, I never considered. That certain equations were being made, certain colors and tonal values being locked away in my visual memory which could later be opened by the right combination of accumulated experience, I never dreamed. (*VC,* 109)

While she calls the day of Ambrose's suicide her "Day of Lost Options" (*VC*, 224), it is, in fact, a day that opens the most important options of all to Violet. In Plommet Falls, she faces her old demons, resists the diversions that have led her astray in the past, and comes to terms with self and work.

A good example of her ironic self-awareness about the necessity of a new approach is her refusal to play the "normal" female role and flirt with the officer in charge of the investigation into Ambrose's death. When it crosses her mind that the officer represents an option, another digression, however pleasant it might be, she resists giving in to her impulse long enough to know that doing so would "defile the tabernacle to [her] muse" (*VC*, 239).

The Satisfactions of Reality

The suggestion that art is the path Godwin's characters are meant to follow, even if the "art" is not always so literal as is the case with Violet, emerges in the closing image of the musician that Jane Clifford listens to in the dark night after she ends her affair with Gabriel. At the end of *Violet Clay*, Godwin has her protagonist conclude that her original goal, to be an artist, was, in fact, her true goal, and she places Violet in a position to accomplish that.

Violet explains her final state this way: "I knew—if only, please God, I would be allowed to keep my eyes—I would go on painting till the day I died. As long as I could paint . . . even if it was just for myself, I wanted to go on living. . . . I would still go on painting because it was something I had to do and something I thought about all the time and something that made me mean and miserable when I wasn't doing it" (*VC*, 244). In coming to this conclusion, an affirmation of both life and art, Violet signals an opening out in Godwin's work, an expanded perspective and an embracing of life in its limited, imperfect reality. The best life that Jane Clifford desires is, through Violet's story, made possible in the context of the flawed world that leaves Dane Empson and Francesca Bolt essentially disillusioned and defeated.

The suspended state that Jane and Violet live in for most of their stories gives way to a new sense of the world in the later novels. For the women in *A Mother and Two Daughters* and for Justin Stokes in *The Finishing School*, life does mean the "infinite rescues, infinite salvations, infinite new starts" (*VC*, 14) that Violet longs for, but the women in the later novels feel no temptation to freeze themselves in some cliche, some Old Plot, while they wait for such largesse to fall on them like grace as long as they conform to the prescribed image. Godwin's later heroines share Violet's hard-won sense of perspective and proportion and use it to shape their lives as artfully as Violet shapes her breakthrough painting of woman suspended.

Chapter Four

Infinite Rescues, Infinite Salvations, Infinite New Starts

A Mother and Two Daughters and The Finishing School

Nell Strickland, one of the three women who are the protagonists of *A Mother and Two Daughters,* belongs to a book club that reads *The Scarlet Letter.* Before the group's discussion of Hawthorne's novel, Nell speaks with her daughter Cate, another of the book's protagonists, who is an English professor at a small midwestern college when the novel begins. Cate tells her mother that "The main thing to remember about *The Scarlet Letter* . . . is that it asks the very crucial question 'Can the individual spirit survive the society in which it has to live?' "[1] In *Violet Clay* Godwin establishes that the individual spirit of her typical character can survive, but the novel ends without subjecting the survivor to the context of her society. In *A Mother and Two Daughters* and *The Finishing School,* Godwin examines in rich detail the lives of varied women of strong individual spirit who do move in clearly defined social contexts. In so doing, she continues to broaden the context of her fiction and to refine the themes and motifs that have always been her trademarks.

Kicking over Old-Guard Traces

As with the two novels that precede it, the plot of *A Mother and Two Daughters* opens with the death of a family member, in this case Leonard Strickland, husband to Nell and father to Cate and her sister, Lydia. The opening chapter, in which Leonard's death occurs, is called "The Old Guard," and in it Godwin sets up the challenge for her three protagonists. Can they move forward? Can they "rescue" themselves? Can they draw on resources they have not previously been obliged to tap? Can they discover salvations in the midst of complications that arise, in part because of the patriarch's death and in part because of the inherent complexities of being female in a time when the old guard and its guardians are disappearing? Can Nell, Cate, and Lydia make new starts?

In the opening pages Theodora Blount, the grande dame of the old guard, expresses the problems inherent in being a "new-fashioned" woman. She says, "I'm all for tough, independent womanhood, you know me, but there's a limit to the traces anybody can kick over, I don't care how privileged or intelligent she is. . . . Nobody can live on the edge of possibility forever, especially not women. Lord knows it's not fair, but a middle-aged woman with no *base* attracts more pity and censure than her male counterpart" (*MTD*, 15–16). As the stories in this novel and those in *The Finishing School* unfold, Godwin explores the validity of Theodora's assessment, and her characters negotiate with themselves and their world to determine exactly which traces they can and should kick over. Through their struggles and their eventual growth, Godwin demonstrates that the edge of possibility can be pushed further and further outward without sacrificing the essential elements of the foundation from which her characters spring.

In *A Mother and Two Daughters* the image of foundations is largely male dominated. Leonard Strickland, an attorney, was locally famous for winning a case involving faulty construction in the city's new bus station with this persuasive closing argument: "If we cannot trust our foundations, what *can* we trust?" (*MTD*, 23). Yet his death sets the novel in motion, and his representative in the next generation, his son-in-law Max, is in the process of being divorced by Lydia. As firmly convinced as Max is that the old guard is right, is the provider of stability and justice, he senses that the stable world that he believes in and works to maintain is passing. When Walter Cronkite ends the evening news with his confident "That's the way it is," Max hears inescapable change beneath the certainty.

Like his father-in-law, Max believes in family as "the bulwark of a moral and stable world" (*MTD*, 54), but he finds himself sleeping separate from his wife. In addition to his impending separation from Lydia and the disruption of his relationship with his two adolescent sons, he finds himself irritated by Cate. To Max, she represents the irresponsible and negative attitudes that have undermined his world and made the old guard a thing of the past. Watching her in her parents' home, he thinks: "The 'Revolution,' that pet word of his sister-in-law, was . . . for many young people down through the ages just a timely carte blanche to abandon the slow and diligent task of making something of themselves and to go out in the open air with their friends and make trouble" (*MTD*, 59).

Cate, Lydia, and even Nell do make trouble of various kinds for themselves and others in the months following Leonard's death, but it is not the irresponsible dalliance that Max imagines. All three women are working toward transformations of self that include recognition of and respect for their pasts and their past selves. The success and power of their progress can be measured by the impact that it has on others, both the lovers, friends, children intimately connected to their lives and those further toward the periphery—secondary characters and strangers whose lives they influence. Like Hawthorne's Hester Prynne, these women slowly and quietly move their social circle toward the future. The novel's epilogue replaces the shattered image of the nuclear family mourning the loss of its patriarch with a fluid and vibrant extended family, presided over by Cate, in many ways the least likely nurturer among them.

The setting of *A Mother and Two Daughters,* Mountain City, North Carolina, is very similar to the unnamed southern city to which Jane Clifford returns in *The Odd Woman* (Mountain City will also serve as the setting for *A Southern Family*), and the phrase "the mother and her two daughters" appears in the earlier novel in a scene in which Jane and her sister Emily sit in a childhood room and talk with their mother (*OW,* 92). But *A Mother and Two Daughters* is a very different novel than *The Odd Woman.* As its title suggests, Godwin's first novel in which the focus is not primarily on an individual female has multiple protagonists.

Cate is a "typical" Godwin woman, and in terms of pages devoted to her and narrator involvement, she is the central figure, but extensive sections are also devoted to both Nell and Lydia, who in earlier works would have been secondary characters instead of protagonists. In addition to examining their relationships with Cate, these sections develop Nell and Lydia separate from those relationships, giving them an autonomy that distinguishes them from important secondary characters, such as Cameron Bolt and Gabriel Weeks. In addition, their independent perspectives enhance our understanding of the standard protagonist figure, making her both more sympathetic and more admirable than she can be when her own limited view is the only one available or when the outside perspective is distorted as it is in the case of Cameron Bolt.

Part 1 of *A Mother and Two Daughters* includes chapters 1 through 3; in addition to "The Old Guard," there are chapters entitled "The Sisters" and "Family Business." This opening section establishes the status quo of the Strickland family in light of Leonard's death. The epigraph to the section, from D. H. Lawrence's "Dies Irae," sets up the strong sense of loss that permeates this portion of the book, but it also indicates the hope that is its ultimate message: "Our epoch is over, a cycle of evolution is finished, our activity has lost its meaning, we are ghosts, we are seed" (*MTD,* 1).

Part 2, the longest, opens with an epigraph from the *I Ching:* "The Chinese character *ku* represents a bowl in whose contents worms are breeding. This means decay. It has come about because the gentle indifference of the lower trigram has come together with the rigid inertia of the upper, and the result is stagnation. Since this implies guilt, the conditions embody a demand for removal of the cause. Hence the meaning of the hexagram is not simply 'what has been spoiled' but 'work on what has been spoiled' " (*MTD*, 83). Thus, it is appropriate that this section, chapters 4 through 8, be the longest. It presents the three women at work on the spoilage of their lives.

Chapters 9 through 11 make up part 3, in which the three women who have been dealing independently with the conflicts in their separate lives are brought together again for the first time since Leonard Strickland's death. Godwin again uses an epigraph from Lawrence, this one from "Be Still!":

> The only thing to be done, now
> now that the waves of our undoing have begun
> to strike on us is to contain ourselves.
>
> To keep still, and let the wreckage of ourselves go. (*MTD*, 321)

The resolutions that arise from their confrontation, both the release and the restraint that the situation involves, lead to the affirmation of the epilogue, with its optimistic epigraph from Ralph Waldo Emerson's "Success": "We are not strong by our power to penetrate, but by our relatedness. The world is enlarged for us, not by new objects, but by finding more affinities and potencies in those we have" (*MTD*, 523).

These epigraphs serve as a coda for the novel's structure in that they summarize the progress of the three women from the despair of the opening section, through the struggle to redefine self and context in the second part, into the resolution and acceptance of part 3, culminating in the thematic statement of the epilogue, in which the best parts of the solid foundation built by Leonard Strickland are woven into a vibrant new sense of self, family, and society, as designed and executed by his wife and their daughters.

Nell Strickland grows up motherless, and in times of crisis in her young life she sometimes longed for an "Ideal Mother" (*MTD*, 168), someone to provide her with the wisdom to rest secure in her decisions. Nell is a practical woman, however, and knows that the Ideal is not always available. In very different ways, each of her daughters also longs for the Ideal. In Cate, that longing is for a social idealism, a world in which justice and freedom are

sacredly preserved and accessible to all and in which her own heroic efforts
on behalf of these principles are recognized and suitably rewarded. For
Lydia the Ideal is more personal. She wants an ordered and principled life in
which her diligence and preparedness guarantee that disaster will not occur.

By the novel's epilogue, all three women have come to share in and reaffirm a conclusion Nell reached early in her motherless life: "in the absence of
the Ideal—which was usually not to be found when you most needed it—
you had to rely on your instincts and common sense" (MTD, 168). Using
those tools, ones traditionally granted to females, the healing and transformation of the plot are made possible.

Mother on the Verge of Independent Life

Nell is in many ways an outsider in the old guard of Mountain City. Her
entree to that very closed society is her marriage to Leonard. Before that, she
was not only an orphan, lacking the bloodline to belong, but also a working
woman, a nurse who is defiled by a cruel doctor in an elevator. Thus, she is
disqualified by loss of virtue and by having to earn her living. Given auto-
matic access through her marriage, she has the outside observer's power
even as she participates in the group and the ironic stance that often comes
as a by-product of such power. While the outer evidence of her life makes
her more like Lydia than Cate, this sense of herself as an outsider, "observant
and occasionally satiric" (MTD, 3), indicates that she is also like her elder
daughter. Nell is not so much a "Southern Lady" as she is an "unsocialized
observer who [has] masqueraded adequately since puberty as a 'Southern
Lady' " (MTD, 6).

One of the problems facing Nell after Leonard's death involves her latent
anger at the scene represented by the old guard. She does not know if she
can tolerate the game playing and posturing that permeate that environment without giving into the sarcasm that is her natural mode, without revealing the cynicism that she had hidden so well for all those years under
Leonard's moderating influence.

The essence of her initial attraction to Leonard was that moderating influence. Her first vision of him came when she was standing on a balcony at
the hospital where she worked. She had just been assaulted by the deft sur-
geon's hands of Dr. Grady Moultrie, a man who introduces her to a passion
that terrifies her without allowing her the pleasure of culmination. Nor will
Moultrie allow her to use her skilled hands on the temple of his body. She is
forbidden to touch; she must succumb passively to his groping toward
whatever pleasure he seeks.

Shut off from the natural outlet of sexual intercourse, her passion finds release in the affinity for sarcasm and cynicism she shares with Moultrie. Her relationship with him transforms Nell into a woman she is afraid of:

> Nell startled herself by her talent for verbal abuse. Before Grady Moultrie, she had *thought* in critical patterns, using these patterns to figure things out for herself (and, in some cases, to anesthetize some pain inflicted by society), but now she heard herself expressing aloud the most scathing configurations of insults in a voice that sounded strange. It came out of her, this dangerously calm, lower-pitched voice, from depths only the little doctor had managed to tap. The strangest thing was, Nell didn't feel all *that* strongly, either way, about these people and institutions she so brilliantly reviled in the presence of her new friend; it was a form of flirtation in which they indulged, she somehow knew that. (*MTD*, 162)

The same horror attends her sexual response to Moultrie. Nell thinks of it as a "sexual thralldom" (*MTD*, 174), and even though she resents the double standard that is inherent in their relationship, she allows herself to continue in this precarious state, partly because of the power of her passion and partly out of fear: "He pushed her hand away and continued to go where he liked with *his* hands. She was angry and humiliated. What was going on here? When he said "mustn't touch," did he mean until they were married? Or never? She didn't even consider asking him. She was afraid he might turn his famous sarcasm on her" (*MTD*, 163).

From the cruel irony of their final encounter in the elevator, when he strips Nell of her technical virginity without providing her with the attending joy of intercourse, she rushes to the balcony, sick with disgust and anger. When Leonard sees her, he sees a beautiful young woman full of an energy and a spirit that he admires. When she sees Leonard, she sees the opposite of Grady Moultrie—a gentle, stable man. His attraction for her is that he appears to be a man "who had never had a scornful thought in his life" (*MTD*, 166). From the cynicism that dominates her perspective when she is with Moultrie, she flees to the camp of life-affirmers that Leonard personifies, and for the five decades of their marriage, their life is precisely what she chose when she chose Leonard: safe, respectable, affirming of all the standard values of the old guard. Sex with Leonard is also the counterpoint to what she had known with Moultrie. It is, for them, a matter of "trusting *assumption*" (*MTD*, 168).

Of course, Leonard's death ends that assumption, and without him Nell's independent self begins to reemerge. She questions whether the isolated safety of the world Leonard created for her and the girls was too se-

cure, too unrealistic. As she and her daughters struggle to face the world
without the safety net of Leonard's rock-hard stability, she wonders about
their fitness for the conflicts they will now face alone. Still, she knows that
she chose that life, that she came to him seeking refuge from a self that was
dangerously close to the edges that Theodora Blount sees as inappropriate
for women. Her daughters know nothing of the true story of their parents'
meeting, nothing about their mother's anger and humiliation that led to the
passionate nature that attracted their father from his vantage point on the
sidewalk below her. It is Leonard's myth of that meeting that has become
the family "truth," and only after his death does Nell begin to wonder about
the wisdom of allowing herself and her daughters to live in an idealized
myth of self and family.

Fifteen years before Leonard's death, Nell faces a turning point when she
sees her first age spot. The small mark on her hand raises the inevitable
questions of aging and mortality that all people confront at different times
in various circumstances. After lamenting her diminishing physical beauty
for a brief time, Nell chooses to look at the flowers in her garden, signs of
continuing growth and life, rather than at her own reflection. By making
such a decision, she not only allows herself to go forward with this next stage
of her life but also reaffirms the choice she made when she decided to marry
Leonard. The Nell of the Moultrie affair would, if confronted with her own
mortality, probably give in to the harsh cynicism of self-deprecation, but
Nell Strickland can continue to look outward with hope, with a positive
rather than a negative eye.

It is also in her garden that she first realizes that she can enjoy her life
after Leonard's death. Her recognition that she is going to live and experience new joys is, in some ways, similar to Jane Clifford's explanation of solitude in *The Odd Woman*. Nell, who has been for 50 years a most married
woman, finds a similar solace in her new independent life. There is, however, a peace and tranquility in her solitude that is not necessarily part of
Jane Clifford's experience. That ease about her condition is in part a feature
of her longer life, in part a result of having had about her those people without whom one feels one cannot live while Jane is still searching for such people. In fact, this stage of Nell's life is complicated more by people who seem
to need her than it is by her need for people. One of the ironies of her relationship with her daughters after Leonard's death is the ill-timed nature of
their need for her.

When Cate and Lydia were younger and Nell truly wanted to "mother"
them, they were always too busy planning "the racy lines of [their] idealistic
young plot[s]" (*MTD*, 326) to stand still for Nell's ministrations or advice.

Now as her adult daughters face the crises of their midlives, they demand the mothering they ignored or rejected earlier just as Nell wants the freedom of her own plot. By meshing this conflict within Nell with Lydia's struggle to be the best possible mother to her teenaged sons during the difficult months after her separation from Max and Cate's decision to have an abortion in the months just before her fortieth birthday, Godwin explores in depth for the first time the complexities of being a mother—or of choosing not to be. Because she treats those issues across the spectrum of age and philosophies that these three women embody, the theme of mother and child relationships begun in earlier works reaches a new breadth and importance in *A Mother and Two Daughters.*

Nell has a dream about Cate that serves as a metaphor for the difficulties inherent in motherhood. She dreams that Cate, with the head of an adult but the body of a baby, is swimming too far from shore. In the dream Nell wants to warn her daughter of the danger she faces but fears that the warning will destroy the illusion that is keeping Cate afloat. Much of what Nell must decide about her daughters during the months that follow their father's death involves the paradox of this dream. She must decide how much truth they can bear without the illusions that are their foundations shattering. It is a delicate decision, and one that must be made time and again. At the same time, Nell must not let the urge to keep her children afloat interfere with her desire to live her own life, have her own plot.

Another intricacy of Nell's relationship with her daughters recalls an image from *The Scarlet Letter.* Hawthorne describes Hester Prynne as moving within an almost mystical field of energy or force that forms a circle around her. No one, not even someone who wishes to help Hester or to soothe the pain of her journey through life, can penetrate this magical field of Hester-ness. Nell feels much the same way about Cate. She cannot penetrate her daughter's Cate-ness and find the best way to help or know what to give. The essence of Cate's personality has been a major puzzle in Nell's life, and only at the novel's end, when she is able to offer her homeless daughter shelter and money, does she feel sure enough about the rightness of that gesture to explain her philosophy of life to her child.

When Cate protests her mother's offer, Nell asserts that philosophy with forthrightness and eloquence: "When you are alive, you do what you *can* do. That's the duty, that's the privilege of the living. I'm not sure the rest matters very much. If you love me, if you honor me at all, you will accept what I offer out of love—and because I *have* it to offer. Otherwise . . . what has it all been *for?*" (*MTD,* 474). Cate accepts. Instead of accompanying Cate to Mountain City, Nell goes to nurse her dying friend Merle, with whom she has been reunited during a vacation to Ocracoke, which brings the Strickland women together for the first time since the funeral. Thus, her gift is offered and accepted without compromising in any significant way the independence or integrity of either woman.

Through the seemingly selfless act of aiding her sick friend (really an acquaintance with whom she has been out of touch for almost half a century), Nell not only succeeds in helping Cate without having to mother her but also lays the foundation for her personal new start. Taking care of Merle persuades her to return to nursing, and after Merle's death she falls in love with and eventually marries Marcus, her husband, an Episcopalian priest.

This late-life marriage opens up a whole new sense of what love can be for Nell. Unlike Leonard, Marcus wants to conduct his mental life in her presence. Leonard lived a separate life in his study and his office; Marcus reads in bed, his life of the mind integrated with his love for her. The project toward which Marcus directs his mental energies is a "philosophy that could reconcile all the disturbing new developments in the world with his deeply felt traditions" (*MTD,* 563). For Nell, their marriage and her return to her profession are embodiments of her success in establishing a philosophy that does reconcile the disturbing elements of the new with the best of the old traditions.

In conjunction with the philosophical symbolism of her marriage and her new life, Nell finds her physical being reawakened. She is amazed at the sexual aspect of her life with Marcus, and during the family party that is the scene of the epilogue, listening to her grandson's band play, she finds herself flushed and excited at the memory of their intimacy. Such a joyous acceptance of one's sexuality is new to Godwin's females, and giving that experience to a character of Nell's age, one who began her sexual life in such a negative way, is a fine example of the novel's motif of infinite rescues, salvations, and starts. That Lydia, the more repressed and sexually inhibited of Nell's daughters, also experiences a sexual awakening during the novel further demonstrates a new sense of peace and affirmation in Godwin's female characters.

What about the Questions You Can't Memorize Answers For?

When Lydia leaves her thoroughly respectable marriage to Max Mansfield, she leaves behind a sexual relationship defined by what she sees as a sportsmanlike attitude on her part and Max's. They have participated in their sexual life willingly and good-heartedly, but the barriers that separate individuals have never been penetrated or dissolved, an arrangement that has, finally, been appropriate for them both. Lydia first meets Stanley Edelman, the man who will become her long-term lover, while she is swimming; thus, their first vision of one another is sensual, and they have little of their physical selves to hide. Still, they approach their relationship at "a decorously sensual pace" (*MTD*, 122) that recalls the physical relationship of Jane Clifford and Gabriel Weeks in *The Odd Woman*.

Their relationship, however, moves beyond their decorous beginning, beyond what Jane and Gabriel have, what Lydia and Max had in their marriage. With Stanley, Lydia crosses a threshold that means that she cannot remain separate. She experiences the enormous power of sex to transform and unite, and, despite her hesitation and fear, she finds that she cannot choose to turn back from that power and joy. She is fully conscious of the change that her relationship with Stanley represents and finds herself able to articulate that change for herself in a way that she would have been unable to do earlier:

[Stanley] wanted her now in a way she had not been wanted before. . . . [H]e was not going to tolerate the little barrier she always left, at these times. Max had tolerated it; he had approved of it, she believed. He had one himself, so they could engage sportingly, with matching handicaps. . . . But this man was not being decorous or sportsmanlike; he was going down willingly into those dark, swirling currents of pure feeling where you could lose yourself. He wanted her to let go completely and be swept away in his waves of ardor. His need for her was so great that he wasn't going to let her reserve one tiny molecule of dry self from the torrent. They'd go down together or not at all. (*MTD*, 134)

There is a danger in the power of such intense physical love, of course. Lydia could find her quest for a new life derailed by the sort of sexual thralldom that almost drove her mother into a negative way of life during her affair with Grady Moultrie. Just as Nell chose Leonard as a counter to her own sarcastic, cynical nature, however, Lydia's choice of Stanley—and she does consciously select him and orchestrate their initial connection—represents a new concept of love for Lydia.

Lydia just as consciously selects Max as her husband while she is a college freshman, drops out of school, marries, and becomes a traditional supportive spouse, effortlessly moving her life onto the well-grooved tracks of the old guard's ways. After she leaves Max, she returns to college and finds herself amazed that her old study habits of memorizing and skillfully repeating what her teachers have told her are the "right" answers will no longer work. In college her teachers demand that she think and come up with answers on her own and that she accept the uncertain nature of most of the answers she eventually settles on.

Her most challenging teacher is a black woman, Renee Peverell-Watson. In Renee's class on the History of Female Consciousness, Lydia takes on the challenging task of defining Eros. As she works on her paper, she is troubled because she does not find a definition that suits her personal sense of Eros. Then Renee guides her to Socrates and his idea of love as a striving toward what one lacks. In this light Lydia's relationship with Stanley mirrors her mother's relationship with Leonard. Leonard embodied the affirming, generous spirit that Nell felt she lacked; Stanley is the passionate, unreserved self that Lydia has kept in check for so long. Her marriage to Max was a striving toward the known, the familiar, because Max is a reproduction of her father. If she accepts the Socratic definition of Eros, then, Max was the wrong man for her since she herself does not lack for the qualities that most define him and her father. In Stanley she finds a different man and, in so doing, opens herself to the possibilities of true Eros because Stanley provides her access to those aspects of herself that have been unexplored.

Lydia, of course, does not know of her mother's relationship with Moultrie or of the thinking behind her choice of Leonard. She has only the revised family version of the myth of Nell and Leonard. But at some subconscious level Lydia has an inkling of her mother's passionate nature and her understanding of all sides of Eros. Lydia recognizes that it is she, not Nell, who would be unable to bear Nell's knowing about the passionate nature of her relationship with Stanley. Loving Stanley does not alter the essence of Lydia's character. The old Lydia does not disappear. Her newly awakened self modifies to some degree that essential nature. It makes her more fully alive, but she still operates out of a strong sense of what is right for her and for others.

The forms and conventions that Nell views with an ironic eye and that so irritate Cate that she constantly throws herself against them are, to Lydia, ultimately freeing. She sees conforming to expectations as giving her distance from the society in which she lives, and with that distance comes a degree of control over what others think of her. In her new life she must face the important question of why she should care what others think, but she has never felt that she was in the power of those others. When she first meets Mary McGregor Turnbull, the hostess of the cooking show that Lydia will eventually take over and transform, she is struck by the kind of power that comes to such old-guard women from the arrogance of knowing who they are and that they are right.

Despite her sense of power and freedom that comes from having always followed the forms prescribed by her society, Lydia realizes that her habit of napping indicates that she has not had a life that would make her want to stay awake. She has always prided herself that she could indulge in the luxury of napping because she was more efficient than others and accomplished more in less time. As she faces the crisis of ending her marriage and the new challenges of school, career, and her affair with Stanley, in addition to the continuing demands of motherhood, she has to come to terms with the fact that her naps were, by and large, escape from a life that did not stimulate or challenge her.

In her late thirties when the novel begins, Lydia senses one evening as she shares a bowl of popcorn with her younger son, Dickie, that she has finally passed her "starting point" (*MTD,* 151). She has been studying while Dickie plays music that he has composed; earlier in the day she has known the pleasures of Stanley's bed. One indication of her having moved beyond her starting point is that her new life allows her to be open to feelings—the sensual beauty of Dickie's music, the intensity of her new passion—whereas the old Lydia's control mechanism was to amass facts against her feelings. The new Lydia uses the facts that her studies lead her to as illumination for her feelings, old and new, as a way to come to terms with and understand those feelings. Her world need no longer be divided into isolated camps of reasoners versus feelers. Beyond her starting point is a place where both camps can mingle and learn from each other, where the individual can nurture and develop both aspects of herself.

Lydia reveals her new sense of herself to Stanley: "I don't know what it is yet . . . only I know it's going to make me more alive than ever. I will be living a life in which I do something that's important. It will be something I can do well and care about doing." (*MTD,* 264)

But her awakening and her new sense of her own potential is not without its complications. Her victory does not come without further struggle and doubt. Lying in bed with Stanley, Lydia suddenly sees her older son, Leo, and seeing Leo she begins to think of Stanley's mother. The complexities of modern life, of being the mother of teenaged sons and lying well satisfied in her lover's bed, certainly collide with the forms and conventions that Lydia has willingly accepted and adhered to all her life. She reacts physically to the incongruities: "All these new juxtapositions made her stomach lurch" (*MTD,* 132).

There is a paradox inherent in Lydia's newfound sense of optimism about

herself and her potential. For the first time in her life, she must deal with
ambiguity. What fuels her new sense of herself also confuses her; what she
wants—freedom to change and continued acceptance and respect—
demands that others change with her, at least enough to modify or expand
the grounds on which they grant her the respect that is essential to her.
Periodically, the difficulty of what confronts her unsettles Lydia:

She was overwhelmed by the blurring of lines that had suddenly complicated her
new life, the life she had intended to have control over. She didn't know where anything fitted, with all these new developments, and she was not going to know as
long as Stanley kept melting her down with kisses. He turned *her* into a blur. . . .
She began to sob with frustration. All these demands on her, it was too much. Why
couldn't life be simpler? (*MTD*, 270)

Lydia's question again brings up the central issue of *The Scarlet Letter* in
that Lydia must, like Hester, negotiate the terms of her progress in a way
that moves her community with her. Like Hester, Lydia chooses the context
of society and must have her freedom within its constraints.

Godwin creates a subplot involving Lydia's older son, Leo, and his girl-
friend, Cookie, to demonstrate the complex nature of Lydia's relationship
with her society. Leo breaks up with Cookie on a matter of principle, Cookie
threatens suicide and does make a very half-hearted attempt, and suddenly
their teenaged friends as well as some parents and teachers cast Leo as the
villain. He finds himself ostracized and confused, and his mother shares his
confusion. Although Lydia is more acutely aware than her son of the staged
melodramatic quality of both Cookie's actions and the public response to
them and even of Leo's tormented reaction to his isolation, she does not understand why he should be punished or censured for trying to live honora-
bly by his stated convictions. He warned Cookie about how he felt and
made clear the consequences; then he followed through. Lydia believes,
however unlikely it is to be borne out, that the person, especially the young
person, who tries to live by his own lights with dignity and without ostenta-
tion should not suffer.

Lydia is a very good mother, perhaps the best mother in all of Godwin's
fiction with the exception of her own mother, Nell. She takes Leo on his
own terms and deals with him gently and effectively. Eventually, the solution to his problem grows out of the solution to Lydia's problem in that he
chooses to leave his North Carolina high school for an English boarding
school. There he meets and eventually marries Renee's daughter. Even as

Lydia helps her son, however, she also uses his experience as an analogue for her own struggles involving Cate, Max, and Stanley.

All her life she has felt that her older sister gets more attention and more reward for subversive or petulant behavior than she does for reasonable, responsible behavior. Thus, Cookie's coming out the "winner" in the conflict with Leo brings to the surface all those old feelings about her sister and their growing up. Even now, it seems to Lydia, their mother expends more energy worrying about Cate and the quality of Cate's life than she does about Lydia and her life. The guilt Lydia feels about ending her marriage for what she fears some people must see as selfish reasons—her own needs—also feeds into her response to Leo's dilemma, and she begins to feel as unfairly accused as her son. (These feelings contain the same exaggerated melodrama as the teenage love plot in that Lydia's sense of guilt and disgrace is grossly exaggerated. When she and Stanley run into Max and Lizzie Broadbelt, the young woman who becomes Max's second wife, leaving a movie before the divorce is official, Lydia gets almost hysterical about what Max will think of her, even though he seems completely unfazed by the meeting.) Even at the end of the novel, after years together and despite her profound love for him, Lydia will not marry Stanley because doing so would somehow violate the principle of their coming together in the first place.

During the community uproar about Leo and Cookie, all these emotions about her new life and how it affects what others think of her collide in Lydia and cause her to call into question both herself and the new life.

Despite an inescapable dependence on a system, an organized structure, a framework for her life, Lydia is committed to the new goal of living a life that makes her feel alive, that keeps her awake and allows her to do what she is good at doing. Renee's boyfriend, Calvin Edwards, invites Lydia to view a taping of Mary McGregor Turnbull's cooking show, for which he is producer. Lydia takes Leo with her, and her son is amazed that Lydia jumps in and goes on the show as a cohost without any preparation or warning. Moreover, she does the job beautifully, and the risk pays off. Television eventually becomes part of her career, the thing that is important and that she does well.

When Leo questions his mother about why she took the chance and how she had the courage, she tells him that it was a matter of motion, openness, meeting challenges so that she would stay on the new track she has laid for herself, a track headed toward a life without regrets. Lydia, asleep for so long, finally awakens, and though she never really leaves the rails laid out by the old guard ("Lydia would not go off the rails. It was not in her"[*MTD*, 21]), she expands the territory into which those rails can carry her.

All her life Lydia has believed that her unfailing dependability is the key to earning her family's respect. She carries that belief into her new life. Stanley, who loves her very much, comes to believe that there is also inherent in Lydia an unhappiness that springs from the world's inability to move fast enough and far enough in its progress toward the ideal order that she works so hard to attain in herself. Marcus Chapin sees the younger of his stepdaughters as a model of a "formidable sense of responsibility," but he also comes to appreciate that Lydia is "softer than even she suspected" (*MTD,* 561).

By making Lydia a complex combination of responsibility and independence, frustration and resentment and true commitment to making herself and the world better, formidability and softness, Godwin recognizes the integrity of a new kind of female character for her. In addition, she brings Lydia and Cate, who more clearly represents the usual Godwin woman, to a real respect for each other by novel's end. Theirs is her most thoroughly explored relationship between women who might be called peers and does much to enrich what has been a somewhat singular view of women of their age and circumstances.

One of God's Experiments

Cate Strickland Galitsky is the typical Godwin protagonist, what her stepfather comes to call one of God's experiments. Like the female characters who have preceded her, Cate longs to create a best life, to fend off ordinariness as if it were a plague. As a result, she has the same extra intensity that the earlier protagonists, to some degree, share. Marcus has a theological explanation for this intensity, carried over from his seminary days. According to one of his professors, "God, in order to become more conscious of Himself, experimented with certain people. These people felt a greater need than others to fling themselves against the world, to let it pierce them and knock them about; they absorbed the world's good or evil, or both, and went on to transmute it into something else. Depending on what the something else was, they became saints or sinners" (*MTD,* 560–61).

In this context, Cate becomes a Hester Prynne figure, someone who transforms the world and inches her society toward a new and better sense of what being human can mean. The most crucial moral decision Cate must make in the novel is whether to abort the child that she conceives while having an affair with Roger Jernigan, the multimillionaire industrialist who is the father of one of her students. Jernigan loves her and offers marriage once he learns she is pregnant. His knowledge is itself, to Cate, a failure on her part to live on her own, by her lights, her principles. In Puritan New England, having a child out of wedlock and refusing to identify the father were the sins that brought forth public outcry against Hester. In the late twentieth century (the novel begins in December of 1978 and covers, including the epilogue, roughly six years in the characters' lives), the moral equivalent, the thing that would generate a similar public outcry, is, perhaps, to abort a child, especially when the father steps forward to accept responsibility.

That Cate chooses to be true to herself and her sense of what is right rather than to do what society would dictate aligns her with Hester and with the entire tradition of women who might be labelled "odd," whether they ever marry or not. It is that tradition of oddity, of God's experimenting, that is Godwin's favorite territory. In Cate she creates her most lively and touching traveler in that territory.

Cate turns 40 during the year following her father's death. The coincidence of his passing, and with him Cate's fondest connection to the old guard, and her own encounter with undeniable middle age causes Cate to doubt her convictions and to question whether the path she has chosen is, in fact, right for her. The emotional crisis of the abortion is compounded by yet another career crisis—the Iowa college where she teaches is closing at the end of the academic year, but she does not find out in time to apply for the "good" positions—and Cate feels a strong temptation to sink into ordinariness. The solid, interesting Jernigan makes the temptation all the stronger. Thus, in one sense, Cate's part of this story is a test of her already strong knowledge of who and what she is. Because she is a Godwin woman, she eventually remains firmly in the camp of the odd, the unordinary, but her growth during the course of the novel gradually modifies and softens the oddities in a way that makes them all the more appealing.

When she considers her dilemma, she is almost always looking at things with an ironic slant, much as her mother might, and very early in the book she recognizes that she has created a catch-22 for herself: "There had been times, lately, when she had yearned to collapse into the protective embrace of someone else's responsibility. But it was too early for that, in one sense; and too late for it, in another" (*MTD*, 36). Stuck with her independence, she falls back on her dominant inherent trait: Cate "[believes] one of the best ways to keep from atrophying [is] to move continually forward to meet the advance of the unpredictable" (*MTD*, 26).

This tendency to motion and to confrontation with the unpredictable can, to some outside observers, appear less than sensible or responsible. Theodora Blount, Cate's godmother, has severed all ties with her god-daughter as a result of Cate's blocking the Lincoln Tunnel during rush hour with the bodies of her preteen students in protest of the U.S. policy in Cambodia. The protest, a matter of principle to Cate, who believed it would be a learning experience for her students, costs her her job as well as her godmother. One measure of the transforming powers of Cate's self is her reunion with Theodora during the closing pages of the novel's last chapter and in the epilogue.

Lydia too questions the behavior pattern that governs her sister's life, even though Cate's resistance to atrophy closely resembles the primary goal of Lydia's new life. Lydia's analysis of Cate's character, kept entirely to herself, relies on heredity and environment to explain her sister's oddity, but she cannot eliminate the possibility of madness as the explanation for much that is otherwise incredible: "Was Cate just the tiniest bit mad? If so, what had done it? Being married to a man who flew U-2s on secret missions? Being married to another man who lived off her salary and took drugs? Was it being alone too much, or . . . had that little spark of madness always been there, glowing at the heart of her personality, waiting for the right event to fan it into flame?" (MTD, 41)

The element of Cate's personality that Lydia fears as madness is to Leonard Strickland a reflection of what he might have become had he not married and had a family. Before he meets Nell, he wants to volunteer in the Spanish Civil War to fight for freedom and justice. In essence, he longs to sacrifice self for principle, to be guided by the spark within that can lead one to the heroic as well as the foolish or insane. From very early on and carrying forward until his death, his older daughter seems to Leonard a more fiery and less prudent version of the young man who longed to plunge into the fray in service of the "right" cause of his time and place.

The relative who talks Leonard out of serving in the war is Uncle Osgood, an eccentric mountain man who represents the family's struggle with itself to some degree. As children, Lydia and Cate are surprised to find their odd uncle at a craft show they attend with their friends. Osgood earns part of his living from the small animals and other creatures that he carves from the wood on his farm. While Lydia, much more concerned about her friends' opinion of her than about her relative's feelings, denies the man, Cate, ever the rebel, embraces him as an act of defiance toward the social expectations that Osgood fails to meet. It is a fitting irony that this odd person Cate champions has given her the father she loves and respects by persuading him to choose the life that leads to Cate and to the stability—the old guard—that Cate chafes against. An additional irony is Cate's finally choosing to settle in the house Osgood leaves her. It is there that the epilogue is set, with the main characters moving forward to new lives but also backward to a part of their past that precedes the staid formality of the old guard.

Just as Osgood and Leonard represent sources for Cate's identity, her nephews, Leo and Dickie, Lydia's sons, serve as gauges for the potential impact of her character. During an evening after the funeral, Cate spends some time with the boys and finds Leo's control and maturity off-putting. To Cate the ideal (or natural) child is an "experimental, healthy insurrectionist" (*MTD,* 64). The paradox of *ideal* and *natural* in her definition apparently escapes Cate, as that contradiction tends to escape Godwin's typical protagonist. Most of these women want to believe that the ideal, attained, is the most natural of conditions for them. Equally ironic, perhaps, is the fact that Cate's definition of the ideal child is a description of her natural self.

With Dickie, she is able to have an interesting conversation. In response to his question about her greatest fear, Cate gives a very honest answer: "The loss of my will to resist" (*MTD,* 65) and goes on to add, "compromise. Cowardice. The sucking pull of the Status Quo" (*MTD,* 66). Clearly, the changes that her sister, Dickie's mother, makes in the novel spring from exactly the same fear, and Lydia's behavior does not seem mad to her or her children or even to outsiders. The difference seems to lie in the way each sister approaches the goal, not in the goal itself. Lydia's unfailing dependability, her contribution to the family, translates, for Cate, into what she comes to suspect is her life's mission: warding off complacency in others.

One defining characteristic in Godwin's development of Cate is her ritual brushing of her hair, a carry-over from the old days and the old ways. Cate's persistent participation in such a ritual confirms that all the rules have not changed for her. She is still a creature of her upbringing, a child of the old guard. The symbolic import of this ritual is reflected in a direct assertion by Cate regarding her attitude toward responsibility and direction in life. She says, "I'm not an aimless or irresponsible person. I simply want to see things for what they are, and I believe in following my instincts—as far as civilization will allow me to." (*MTD,* 77)

In addition to being yet another echo of *The Scarlet Letter,* this expression, coming early in the novel, before Cate meets Roger Jernigan, sets up the crucial conflict she will face. In dealing with her feelings for Jernigan and the moral murkiness of her abortion, the goal she states early on—to see things for what they are and to follow her instincts within society's constraints—comes under the severest possible test.

That Cate experiences such conflicting emotions about the abortion and her relationship with Jernigan demonstrates that she has not left her past

and its values completely behind. If she were merely an irresponsible anar-
chist in regard to social mores and moral values, she would have the abortion without such conflict. In the midst of the separate and independent life
she has established in Iowa (and in the other places she has lived since leaving home), however, she finds herself serving two masters: the past and the
future she envisions for herself.

After she has gone through most of the main events of the novel, Cate explains this vivid sense of her relationship to time using D. H. Lawrence as
her source. Talking to Marcus and Merle, her mother, and Lydia at the
beach house at Ocracoke, Cate echoes the epigraph to part 1 of the novel.
She describes the present as the end of an epoch and contemporary humans
as ghosts going through empty rituals of tradition. Those same humans, according to Lawrence, Cate explains, are also seeds of underground movement toward a new world, the essence of the infinite new starts that Violet
Clay looks for. The source of that potential for new beginnings is "what's
true and living and indestructible in us" (*MTD*, 413). Thus, Cate's life is
designed to bring about a new order just as in her dissertation she interprets
Lawrence's poetry as a design for a new world.

As she considers the consequences of her relationship with Jernigan, the
most important of which is the pregnancy, Cate puts the situation into historical perspective. In the past—say, in the thirteenth century—a woman in
her position, pregnant and unmarried, would have had all her decisions
made for her. There would have been no dilemma; there would also have
been no freedom. When she agrees to spend the weekend before the abortion is scheduled with Jernigan at his castle, a modern-day replica of where
she might have lived, had she been a medieval woman, the romance and the
ease of a dependent life pull strongly at her.

Making love with Jernigan in the castle awakens a primitive side of her
that surprises and puzzles Cate: "She was tired of being conscious and witty
and responsible. She wanted to get down to basics, to take and be taken.
Nevertheless, she was surprised when she heard something like a growl escape from herself" (*MTD*, 239). The responsibility Cate is tired of is different from the responsibility that Lydia prides herself on, a very old-guard
sense of responsible behavior. The burden that Cate bears is a more modern
one; hers is the responsibility that comes from being a twentieth-century
woman who exercises and enjoys the freedom of the new age and, thus,
must face the consequent responsibilities.

Cate meets Jernigan through his son Jody, who plays Dracula in a college production directed by Cate. Because of the associations with Jody
and the play and because she watches a documentary of the Dracula myth

with her nephews while she is home for her father's funeral, Cate finds herself contemplating the lure of this medieval story in connection with her relationship with a man who lives in a castle. While she is a guest at the castle, she stays in Jody's room, which she thinks of as Dracula's bedroom. He has decorated it in a style suitable to a gothic romance, the kind of room one of Violet Clay's cover heroines might live in. The startling growl rises out of Cate in this room, and the atmosphere's power is almost hypnotic, temporarily.

The intellectual side of Cate determines that the lure of the Dracula myth is sexual but that the story is also attractive because of its promise of effortless and easy transformation from an outside source. Ultimately, giving oneself up to such a force is antithetical to Cate's nature. She works on perpetually transforming herself and then using her enhanced powers to transform the world around her. She will not marry Jernigan and move into his castle because doing so would mean sacrificing her freedom to define herself along with ridding herself of the burdens of her responsibilities.

Cate suspects the body of a subtle kind of treachery, much as Violet Clay's body betrays her on her first day in New York when she has to destroy part of her portfolio to cope with the onset of her menstrual period. Before she becomes pregnant, Cate enjoys sex with Jernigan; after she conceives, she loses all appetite for sex. This situation seems unfair to her: "It appalled her that her few times of pleasure and fellow comfort with Jernigan should have landed her in such murky moral waters" (*MTD,* 199). Because she is facing her fortieth birthday at the same time she faces the unexpected pregnancy, the thought of menopause also crosses her mind, and she imagines it as a freeing experience, one that enables a woman to be herself and nothing else.

Once her pregnancy is confirmed, she makes herself a promise that she will not tell Jernigan. The almost immediate breaking of her promise indicates the vunerability and the conflict within Cate. Jernigan comes over with a pizza, they fight (Cate later realizes she causes the fight), she loses the control she prides herself on and tells him. This sets up her weekend at the castle, which puts her more important resolve not to have the child to a final test. Her oddly surprising arousal at the romance of the castle is, Cate suspects, another sign of the body's treachery. Her physical self tries to override her emotions and intellect in order to preserve the child by making the world Jernigan offers irresistible.

What Cate sees as her weakness in revealing her secret provides an excellent example of how the novel's multiple points of view enhance the story's meaning and open it up in ways not possible in the earlier work. Having told Jernigan, Cate has a sudden insight into her mother's character, wondering what stories might lie behind the remarkable control of Nell's life. If the novel were limited to Cate's perspective, the reader would never know the answer to that question, but because Godwin moves into Nell's point of view two chapters later, the reader hears some of those stories, most notably the one about Nell's relationship with Moultrie and its connection to her marriage and her control. Cate's intuitive sense that such stories do exist in her mother's experience raises another important question, one that will eventually generate the story in *A Southern Family*. Suddenly feeling that she understands her mother in a way that hasn't been possible before, Cate wonders why it is that family relationships can be penetrated and understood only in hindsight.

Although hindsight does not call her decision to refuse Jernigan's proposal into question, it does cause her to question herself and her goals: "What more *did* she want? . . . That was the trouble. She couldn't think of what more she did want, she could only know what she didn't want. . . . though you knew your life was not perfect, your hopes for the future lay in keeping a space ready for what you did want, even though you didn't know what it would be until it came" (*MTD*, 244–45). Having committed herself to such an amorphous but demanding goal, Cate is embracing oddity: choosing to remain unmarried (Gissing's nineteenth-century sense of the word) and choosing to live over the edge of the socially prescribed territory accessible to a well-brought-up southern girl.

The sort of peace that waiting for one's future requires is always, for Cate, in conflict with a rage about others' inability to foresee or work toward the world she envisions. Contemplating Sarah Jane Moore, the woman who tried to shoot Gerald Ford, Cate figures that Moore acted out of fury at Ford's unjustified success and her own impotence to do anything about it. The incident with her students and the Lincoln Tunnel that cost Cate her job demonstrates that her own frustration and rage can lead to actions that ultimately impede rather than contribute to her progress. The novel's plot, after her refusal of Jernigan, forces Cate into situations that bring her closer to the peace necessary to attaining her goal of leaving herself open for the life she wants, that take her in the direction of Hester Prynne instead of Sarah Jane Moore.

In the summer after her father's death in December, Cate packs all her worldly goods into her Volkswagen and heads home, jobless, to accompany her mother and Lydia to the family's summer home on Ocracoke Island, off North Carolina's shore. They are to clean out Leonard's things, but the journey is also spiritual, a way to be in touch with each other and with the essence of their husband and father in a place that was especially dear to him.

By the time this reunion arrives, the reader has gotten to know each of the three women separately and knows the tensions and conflicts that are likely to emerge. Lydia is full of the new confidence that her classes, her affair with Stanley, and her friendship with Renee and Calvin have generated. She will not willingly remain in Cate's shadow, especially since she, too, is a single woman now, with the added responsibility of motherhood, and still as organized and efficient as ever. Cate's sloppy life will irritate Lydia more than ever. Nell, having come to enjoy the solitude of her widowhood and the possibility for having her own plot at last, will not want to be drawn into the conflicts facing each of her daughters or the tension between them. Cate, at a real low point with the college's closing, the abortion, and 40 staring her in the face, will see Lydia's progress as having been financed by Max and her friendship with blacks and sudden interest in female consciousness as easy, cocktail-party liberalism. Both daughters will feel that their mother is not being motherly enough.

For Cate, the trip to Ocracoke and the family cottage, where she is planning to live for the summer while sending out resumes in hopes of finding a job, puts her in a situation that closely parallels Violet Clay's Day of Lost Options. Through the joint carelessness of the sisters, a fire in the fireplace spreads sparks across the roof and ignites it. The ensuing blaze destroys the cabin, symbolically ridding them of an important element of their past and eliminating Cate's last faint hope for her future.

While the cottage burns, Cate walks angrily on the beach during heavy winds. This walk exacts a personal price beyond the loss of the cottage, afflicting her with Bell's palsy, which partially paralyzes her face. The disease, coming as a result of her uncontrolled fury at her sister, serves as a reminder of limitations and limited entitlements to fresh starts. Being stripped of all options, left with nothing except her car, Cate must accept her mother's offer of help. She goes back to the house in Mountain City while her mother accompanies the Chapins to their home to nurse Merle. In Mountain City, Cate reaches a new sense of tranquility that allows her to transform her future and to set her life on course for the world she has long envisioned.

Before she and Nell leave for Ocracoke, Cate tells her mother what that world would be like:

I want to understand . . . I want to be free to conduct my own sustained inquiry into this maddening, fascinating, infuriating world I was born into. I don't particularly want to starve or live in ugly places, and I'd like a few friends, and if I can't teach in a college or university, maybe I can find a *cluster*. . . . They don't even have to be disciples, just a few engaged minds, so I won't go crazy with loneliness. . . . I can forgo the luxuries. . . . though . . . I once thought of them as my simple entitlements. . . .

I think I can forgo the luxuries if I can have the freedom and mobility to investigate things as they are, and maybe call a few truths as I see them, without getting arrested or put away in a madhouse. If I can be allowed to do that for a few more years, I think I will have fulfilled my purpose in life. Oh, and I'd like to keep my health, if possible. (*MTD*, 367–68)

It takes the experience of her trip to Ocracoke to position her so that she can recognize the desired future when it beckons.

As she settles into her childhood home, Cate is symbolically entering an environment that reflects her personality. The house, specifically designed by Leonard to be perfect for his family, is unfortunately not perfectly suited to the lot on which it is built, its environment, the metaphoric equivalent of social context for Cate. Very early in the novel, Godwin has described the problem with the house: "When the wind blew in a certain direction, the house wailed like a banshee. They would have to live with it: the condition was inherent in the incompatibility of the structure and its high lot. . . . As in an old marriage, its disharmonious elements had, through long proximity, adjusted themselves into a semblance of mellowed accord" (*MTD*, 34).

While Cate occupies the house alone, apparently stripped of options, partially paralyzed, adrift, she finally reaches a similar feeling of mellow accord with herself, and that accord within Cate sets up the transmutation of all the characters and conflicts that produces the almost euphoric joy of the epilogue. This transformation within Cate also signals a solidifying of the new strengths in Godwin as an artist and opens the way for a stronger, more generous fiction:

As light ebbed from the room, she felt, with relief and a certain interest, her own resistance merging into the growing obscurity: its hard center seemed to break slowly into fragments and disperse. Resistance to what? It had been her stance for so long that it had become a way of life. She felt her actions, to date, had been paid for. The problems ahead, while they did not solve themselves, seemed to be dissolving, like the light, into the rich, gathering dark. . . . She could not say she felt hopeful, but neither did she miss the hope. . . . As she lay there, not sleeping, but with her breathing growing calmer and deeper, she felt both sentenced and redeemed. And accepted both. (*MTD*, 480–81)

The connection to Hester Prynne's sentencing and redemption and her acceptance of both, which is shared eventually by the community, who come to accept Hester's redeemed and transformed self, is another clear link between Cate and Hawthorne's heroine. The first important gesture of Cate's newly transformed self, after she experiences the relaxing and healing power of her time alone in the family home after the fire at Ocracoke, is to effect a reconciliation between her godmother Theodora and Wickie Lee, a young woman Theodora has taken in.

This reconciliation also leads to a healing of the scars in Cate's relationship with Theodora, who is part of the epilogue's extended "family." Jernigan, too, appears, on new terms that allow Cate her independent life and her feelings for him. The occasion for the party at the cabin that Osgood leaves to Cate is a celebration of Leo's marriage to Renee's daughter, Camilla. The entire family comes, just as they did in the opening section for the funeral. Only now, the group has been expanded through the protagonists' transformations of self and context, and the event is a celebration of growth and newness rather than a lament for something forever lost. The group assembled for the party includes the sisters, Cate and Lydia, and their mother, of course, and Leonard Strickland's grandchildren, Leo and Dickie.

To this "nuclear" family, Godwin adds Marcus Chapin, Nell's new husband; Jernigan and Stanley, the sisters' lovers, both of whom are nonsoutherners and one of whom, Stanley, is a Jew; two blacks, Camilla and Theodora's maid, Azalea, who attended her employer's party that opens the novel as a servant but who is at Cate's house as friend and companion to Theodora, who has recovered from a stroke; Theodora, the epitome of the old guard; Sicca Dowling, a member of Nell's book club and a recovering alcoholic who now lives in Marcus and Nell's basement; Wickie Lee and her family, which includes the child she bore while living with Theodora, her husband and his children from a previous marriage, and a new child on the way; Liza Bee, the child of Max's marriage to Lizzie Broadbelt but largely the responsibility of Lydia and Stanley because of Max's death three months before her birth and Lizzie's demanding career; Heather, a young doctor who shares Cate's house while serving the people of rural Appalachia; and the members of Dickie's band. This motley crew is, in fact, the "cluster" that Cate describes to her mother on the evening before they leave for Ocracoke. The difference is that Cate has changed enough to accept these people for what they are, to engage in an exchange with them that recognizes them on their own terms, as the epigraph from Emerson that begins the epilogue suggests: "We are strong not by our power to penetrate, but by our relatedness. The world is enlarged for us, not by new objects, but by

finding more affinities and potencies in those we have" (*MTD*, 523). The
music of Dickie's group, The Wandering Winds, ends *A Mother and Two
Daughters*, but, unlike the isolated music from afar that ends *The Odd
Woman*, this music connects everyone in this oddly configured group, permeates their separateness, and creates a feeling of unity and optimism that is
not found anywhere else in Godwin's work. The music is a metaphor for the
affinities and potencies that can enlarge the world in which we find
ourselves.

The Danger of Congealing

In *The Scarlet Letter*, Arthur Dimmesdale defines the worst sin as violating the sanctity of the human heart. In a discussion with a Catholic friend,
Cate explores which of all possible sins against the Holy Ghost, "the worst
sin, according to Catholics," is the absolute worst. Her friend believes that it
has "something to do with making a human being despise his own nature,
the nature God [has] given him and that he [has] to live with" (*MTD*,
466). Just as the plot of *A Mother and Two Daughters* moves its characters
toward respect for the essential nature of each individual in their restricted
"society" of family and friends, the story told by Justin Stokes, the first-
person narrator of *The Finishing School*, chronicles her struggle to grow and
to nurture her specialness, her unordinariness, without violating the sanctity
of another's identity or denying others their defining natures. The main vehicle for Justin's growth and her development as a gifted actress possessed
of an acute and individual perspective is Ursula DeVane, a woman she
meets the summer she turns 14. Telling the story when she is 40, the same
age as Cate when she finally "mellows," Justin still finds herself questioning
her treatment of Ursula and wondering whether she did, in fact, deny
Ursula the very integrity of self that she demands at the same time that she
struggled to penetrate the sanctity of Ursula's heart in order to fuel her own
progress.

Early in her brief relationship with Justin, Ursula DeVane provides the
girl with an image that serves as a touchstone in Justin's life. She explains
to Justin that there are two types of people in the world: those who have
congealed, have let their lives trap them in a rigid and ordinary existence,
and those who remain fluid, open to change. Anyone who has read
Godwin's previous novels recognizes Ursula's classification as a statement
of one of Godwin's major themes. The primary struggle of all her protagonists is to avoid what Ursula terms a congealed life. The juxtaposition of
the adult Justin's sensibilities and desires with her memory of the way she

felt and observed the world around her at 14 indicates the ongoing nature of the struggle to remain fluid and provides, for the first time in Godwin's novels, a thorough examination of the origins of this definitive longing in her protagonists.

At 14 Justin is already determined, like her predecessors in Godwin's work, to escape the ordinary, and after moving from her home in Fredericksburg, Virginia, to the village of Clove in rural New York state, she soon spots Ursula as "her best bet in the village"[2] for access to the unordinary. Remembering her first impressions of Ursula years later, she recalls that even before she knew her well, Ursula "fed her mind and stoked her desire for the larger life" (*FS*, 5).

At 40 Justin is a successful actress, the profession that Ursula attempted but abandoned because of family obligations and that Ursula early on identified as right for Justin, who had from childhood demanded "that constant heightening of reality only art can give" (*FS*, 2). As she makes a ritualistic journey back to Clove in her fortieth year to rethink that crucial fourteenth summer, Justin is, in a way, meeting Ursula's original challenge to her to leave the stronghold of her safe life, to forsake all its props, and meet the essence of life head on. In that sense, Justin again uses Ursula and the telling of her story to prevent congealing. Ursula—or, more exactly, Justin's image of her—serves to "stir things up" (*FS*, 4) for Justin, and the telling of the story and the return to the scene of the events are an effort to tend her image of Ursula rather than to find the actual woman.

Where Fourteen Meets Forty

Just as she needed to invent a relationship with Ursula at 14 to escape the horrible conformity and dullness of the archetypal 1950s suburb where she has come to live with her aunt, Mona Mott, and her cousin, Becky, along with her mother and her brother, Jem, after the deaths of her father and her beloved grandparents, at 40 Justin needs to recreate what she and Ursula were to each other. Thus, she demonstrates exactly how well she has learned Ursula's lesson by transforming her mentor's own life into art that serves her need for a heightened reality, again and again. Because she is approaching the age that Ursula was when they met (44), there is a new quality to Justin's vision of the older woman. She comes to a broader sympathy for Ursula's personal needs, begins to see the real woman as well as the myth that she created at 14 and has maintained and embellished ever since.

In her revised version of Ursula, Justin approaches the same opening-out in her perspective that occurs in the characters in *A Mother and Two Daugh-*

ters; she comes to recognize the importance of relatedness and the affinities and potencies that the Emersonian epigraph to the earlier novel celebrates. Her narrative stance also recalls another famous first-person narrator who examines a somewhat unlikable character who has profoundly influenced him. Like Nick Carraway in *The Great Gatsby,* Justin opens her story with a direct statement intended to guide readers' response to Ursula, who might, if events unfolded without the statement, be too unlikable. Just as Fitzgerald's Nick insists that Gatsby is the one who was all right in the end and the others were the foul dust that trailed in his wake, Justin immediately indicates that Ursula is deserving of our sympathy by apologizing for her treatment of the woman: "I'm sorry for the way I behaved at the end. The older I get, the more cruel that behavior seems" (*FS,* 2).

The structure of *The Finishing School* resembles that of Fitzgerald's novel in another way, also. Although Violet Clay is both narrator and central focus of Godwin's other novel in first person, Justin's relationship to the main plot of *The Finishing School* more closely resembles Nick Carraway's relationship to the key events in *The Great Gatsby.* Like Nick, Justin has come to an unfamiliar environment and becomes involved with a local mythic figure. Through observation and peripheral involvement in the events that unfold, like Nick, Justin does undergo growth and change; that progress is then enhanced through the later telling of the story. The big "events" of the novel involve Ursula and her brother, Julian, however, more directly than they do Justin herself.

This is not to say that Justin is without conflict or to suggest that she is not the protagonist of the novel. In many ways, she is the classic Godwin protagonist with the typical conflict made even clearer because of her youth and the overt split in her loyalties between Ursula and her family. Those factions that vie for Justin's loyalty during her fourteenth summer come to stand for larger conflicts that are always integral to Godwin's fiction: the individual versus the group, independence versus dependence, the extraordinary versus the ordinary, or, to use Ursula's image, the fluid versus the congealed. In very straightforward terms Justin feels enormous pressure to choose between the world that she imagines Ursula to represent and the world of Lucas Meadows, the subdivision where her aunt and her cousin live, where every single home features the same picture window with a lamp sitting in the same place, where the ritual of fathers mowing the lawn on Saturday is so entrenched that Eric Mott, Mona's husband from whom she is separated, returns on Saturdays to perform his landscaping duties.

The older Justin who returns to Clove and who tells the story of her summer with Ursula projects herself into Ursula's point of view during that fateful season, and in so doing she realizes that Ursula DeVane saw young Justin—a teenager who had lost father, grandmother, and grandfather in her brief life and who had subsequently been dislocated and brought into a foreign environment to live as a "poor relation" in the home of an aunt she barely knew—as having suffered slight misfortune and inconvenience. On the other hand, Justin sees in retrospect, Ursula saw herself and her family as having lived out a high tragedy, as Sophocles and Ibsen might define tragedy.

Of course, to live high tragedy is to make art of one's life, and the older Justin recognizes the dangers inherent in that enterprise, partly because she (like most of Godwin's heroines) shares that tendency with her mentor. More like Violet Clay in the end than like Ursula DeVane, Justin learns to separate life and art and to let the misfortunes and inconveniences of real life fuel her renderings of tragic heroines on stage. She understands the subtle difference in using the stuff of one's life to make art and staging life itself as art. The odd relationship between Justin and Ursula raises, really for the first time in Godwin's novels, the moral and ethical complexities of the artist's need for using others and their lives as the stuff from which the art is created. Justin and Ursula use each other, and one of the questions the older Justin wants to answer is whether one is more guilty than the other.

The questions about the relationship between life and art that Justin raises are primarily a function of her looking back at events long past and evaluating their influence on the person she is in the present. Even in the past, in the present time of her fourteenth summer, there is a strangely arty feel to the way events unfold, suggesting that Ursula was, in part, directing them, drawing Justin into a major supporting role in the drama of her life. Beyond that is the eerily staged quality of events outside even Ursula's control that take on, in the retelling years later, the qualities of "fiction."

An excellent example from early in the novel of the uncanny resemblance between Justin's life and an artistic rendering of reality is a scene that recalls the clear influence of D. H. Lawrence on *The Perfectionists* and *A Mother and Two Daughters*. Riding her bicycle out Old Clove Road, Justin passes the farm of Abel Cristiana, whose son Ed will later take Justin on her first date. She is brought to a halt by the sight of two horses mating, and their sheer physicality and the enormous sensual power of the scene echo the Laurentian treatment of horses as symbols of sexuality. When Abel Cristiana sees Justin watching his horses, she is so embarrassed that she jumps back on her bike and pedals furiously on down the road, going farther from Lucas Meadows than she has ever gone before, winding up at Ursula's house for the first time.

In isolation, this scene has some of the symbolic import of a "literary" scene, though it is presented as a scene from Justin's "real" experience, what with its echoes of Lawrence, its connection to the boy who will begin Justin's career as a "woman," and its role in carrying Justin toward Ursula and away from her family. By the end of the novel the scene represents the kind of plotting that one usually associates only with fiction and not with real life, for it is Abel Cristiana who plays the pivotal role in the final unwinding of the high tragedy that is Ursula DeVane's life.

Abel is Ursula's lover and the archenemy of the DeVane family. His farm adjoins their property, and in order to survive they are gradually having to sell him pieces of the land that has been in their family for centuries. To her brother, Julian DeVane, Ursula could commit no greater act of betrayal than to consort with Cristiana. Justin is drawn into the situation when she comes on Abel and Ursula having sex in the building that has been her "finishing school" that summer, the place where she and Ursula have met to talk and to imagine together. Because it is almost dark and Justin is out later than she should be, Julian has led Eric Mott, who is looking for his niece, to the finishing school just as Justin realizes what is going on inside the building.

Instead of going to her uncle and Julian without doing anything to reveal what she has discovered, Justin jumps into the pond next to the finishing school. Ursula, believing that Justin cannot swim, jumps in to "save her," and, thus, Julian becomes aware of his beloved and devoted sister's terrible betrayal. Julian hangs himself that night.

The irony of Justin's having moved toward Ursula after having observed Abel's horses mating and then moving away from her, literally as she is taken back to the safety of Lucas Meadows by her uncle and figuratively in that her action is, ultimately, a betrayal of the world Ursula represents, having observed Abel himself "mating" with Ursula brings to the structure of Justin's life, especially that particular summer, the feel of fiction or drama.

That is not the only irony in the scene, by any means. The humiliation of the DeVanes' having had to sell land to Abel Cristiana and Julian's enormously haughty pride about having nothing to do with him suggest an absolute quality to Julian's moral scheme, and his suicide after discovering his sister's connection to their neighbor indicates that Julian is determined to carry that scheme to its logical conclusion. However, the money that comes from the sale of land to the Cristianas is money for the continuation of Julian's own artistic hopes. Ursula abandons her own life and her hopes for escaping the ordinary to return to foster and support her brother's stalled musical career.

To add yet another layer of irony to this scene, Godwin has Ursula confide in Justin the story of the first act in the family tragedy. The DeVanes' mother, engaged in an affair with Julian's music teacher and mentor, was discovered in the act by Ursula, in the very same stone hut that would years later become Justin's finishing school and the place where Justin would discover her mentor and surrogate mother figure again betraying the family by a sexual indiscretion. This story about their mother and her affair with Karl, the music teacher, has been concealed from Julian, just as Ursula's relationship with Abel has. By bearing the burden of the family truth alone, Ursula makes herself a martyr of sorts, which is one way of compensating for the guilt she feels at having betrayed her mother by telling her father about the affair with Karl.

By deciding to jump into the pond and draw Eric Mott and Julian to the scene, Justin mirrors Ursula's decision to reveal her mother's infidelity. That action returns Justin to the safety of the known world, makes her a child a little longer, but also instills in her a lingering sense of guilt, much like Ursula's own sense of guilt about what she did when she discovered her mother and, the older Justin has to assume, about her ongoing affair with Abel. This climactic episode that shatters the summer for Justin also raises serious questions in her mind about the way that people deal with one another. Justin feels trapped in the plot of Ursula's life, but at the same time she realizes that she was using Ursula in a youthful effort to seize control on her own plot, to shape it toward the heightened reality that the DeVanes represent for her. In this exchange in which people use parts of others for their own needs while discarding the inconvenient or contradictory parts, the whole person is, finally, ignored and the "vibrant, undefinable connection" (*FS*, 103) that produces the affinities and potencies the characters originally seek from their relationship is never realized.

(Readers familiar with Lawrence's *The Rainbow* will, of course, be aware of the echoes in Ursula's and Cristiana's names and the key role of the pond in *The Finishing School*. Lawrence has clearly been a major influence on Godwin, and the connections between the two are an area for fruitful exploration.)

Just as Cate feels that she is somehow representative of both the old and the new, Justin sees herself as a creature of two worlds: the mystical and the pragmatic. One of the things that first draws her to the DeVane house is the sound of Julian's Bach drifting through the woods to Old Clove Road. For Justin, Bach recalls her dead grandfather and the home and way of life she fears are lost to her forever. When she hears Julian playing, the two sides of her nature conspire to lead her to the music: "It was as if, the mystical side of me fancied, the ghost of my grandfather had sent me these snatches of music, traveling faintly through the spring air, to console me. And yet the pragmatic side of me was curious to find out just who in this rural village was playing J. Sanity Bach" (*FS*, 10).

She does explore the source of the music, meets the DeVanes, and spends a summer being swayed by the mystical aura of Ursula and Julian, hoping against hope that she is worthy of the life they hold out to her vivid imagination at the same time she is fully conscious of the more pragmatic reasons for her attraction to this odd, older couple. She is lonely, in a strange place, awash in the ordinariness and mundanity of life in Lucas Meadows. She is also witness to changes in her mother, and she is not sure how well she likes the new woman whom she begins to see. The DeVanes are the most pragmatic alternative, an escape.

The novel's epigraph from Rainer Maria Rilke's *Sonnets to Orpheus*, II. 23 (translated by M. D. Herbert Norton), suggests another dichotomy in Justin's character, for she is, at once, in this novel a young girl and a middle-aged woman. The epigraph emphasizes the similarities in the two selves in terms of desire and sense of loss and perpetual longing: "Anxiously we clamor for a hold,/we, too young sometimes for what is old/and too old for that which never was." When the older Justin tries to recreate the feelings of that summer in Clove, the limitations of her age—she is too old—become apparent to her: "Then the 'cinema' memory takes over. My senses continue on with me, but not my feelings, thoughts, or motivations. I am like an observer at the movies, positioned by the camera behind the eyes of the girl. I can 'see things from her angle,' but I have no access to her mysterious inner workings" (*FS*, 292).

It is also this sense of being too old to recapture fully the deepest mysteries of her young self that intensifies Justin's understanding of Ursula in a way that has been impossible up until her return to Clove at 40. For in that summer of their connection Ursula must have had to conclude that she was too old to connect with the self she had abandoned so long ago, that all her hopes for Justin and all her identification with her young disciple were, finally, no better than the limited cinematic perspective of the older Justin.

Just as Justin uses her image of Ursula to stir herself up at 40, Ursula senses the need for arousal in herself when she meets Justin: "I have reached a time in my life when I need to be refreshed by the unexpected rather than consoled by the stately rhythms of what I know" (*FS*, 18). Even the knowledge of one's limits that comes as a by-product of the refreshment can be an asset for Ursula. One of her most important legacies to Justin is her concept of yearning and its importance to art, love, passion, the best life.

As they are discussing the feelings evoked by Julian's musical interpretation of the Rilke sonnet from which the epigraph is taken, she tells her young friend about the importance of yearning (which much resembles the German concept of *Weltschmerz*): It's more like a *yearning*. The person in the song is really addressing a powerful and constant state of yearning more than he is any real love. It's the state of yearning that torments him, yet he also loves his torment. He *needs* it. Because he understands that being able to feel this yearning so exquisitely is his secret strength" (*FS*, 48). She then goes on to connect this important sense of yearning to art: "That is the power of the artist, you see. If you are an artist, you learn how to trap the yearning and put it where you want it, put it where it goes. That's the secret all true artists come to know" (*FS*, 48).

This lesson is very important to Justin's later development as an actress; it is perhaps the crucial ingredient to her success. But she also draws lines that the DeVanes seem unable or unwilling to draw. She does not, even as a 14-year-old, grant to the artist license to go completely over the boundaries of convention in service to his or her particular yearnings. As much as Justin likes Julian DeVane and as moved as she often is by his playing, she also finds him in violation of norms she cannot relinquish. At 14 she thinks, "The man did seem crazy. Or very insensitive. Ursula DeVane had called it 'an occasional display of impulsiveness' to which an artist was entitled. But, as much as I had liked her, I couldn't excuse him. It seemed to me that artists, if anything, had more of a duty to behave well, because people looked at them more" (*FS*, 27).

This is an important statement in tracing Justin's growth into the responsible and successful artist that she becomes, and it is equally important to understanding Godwin's evolving standards for the artistic life or for any life that strives toward the unordinary. Like Cate in *A Mother and Two Daughters*, Justin works toward a reconciliation of the old and the new, in Justin's case represented by her family and the DeVanes. Thus, it is fitting that her judgment of Julian relates to his treatment of her cousin, Becky. Justin does not really like Becky, nor does she admire what Becky stands for as a child or even as an adult, but she does side with her and the standard family position on this important issue.

Ursula is, however, much more important to Justin than Julian is, and choosing the family over Ursula is naturally more difficult. Justin is a precocious child in many ways, and she is unsettled by her inability to place Ursula as she usually can other adults: There was some indefinable thing in her style . . . that made me unable to 'place' her the way I habitually did adults, either relegating them to their function pertaining to me or judging them with pity or sternness because they had spoiled themselves or been defeated by life in some visible way. This woman seemed . . . not judgeable by my usual standards and categories for older people" (*FS*, 13).

Even the older Justin has the same problem with deciding exactly what Ursula DeVane was when she knew her. On her return trip to Clove, Justin learns that Eric Mott was Ursula's lover for a while after that fateful night at the finishing school. That her uncle, the orphan who embraced the IBM corporation as his family, the man who considered Lucas Meadows the epitome of what life could offer, should be a fitting partner for the woman she had idolized confuses Justin all over again. At 40 she thinks, "What was she, really? A brilliant woman, thwarted by family and fate—and self? Or a colorful failure who was able to fascinate a young girl, as well as some married and lonely men in the neighborhood?" (*FS*, 167).

Behind the Picture Windows

One of the ironies of Justin's life after her summer with Ursula is that the women she saw as inferior to her mentor, primarily her mother and her aunt, go on to transform their lives and become successes on their own terms, while Ursula, Justin must assume from details such as Mott's affair with her, remains trapped in the destructive myth of self that she had created and pursued for so long.

Louise Stokes admits to having done only two enterprising things in her entire life prior to the summer she comes to Clove with her children. The first she does as a young visitor at a dance, where she meets Craven Ravenel, a local boy, with whom she wants to dance so badly that she writes his name on her dance card herself, for the important last dance. He so admires her resourcefulness and her beauty that he goes along with the ploy and dances with her. In another example of life's taking on the qualities of fiction, Louise and Justin go to New York City during that key summer and run into Craven Ravenel and his wife at the theater. As fate (or fiction) would have it, the Ravenel marriage is in trouble; Craven and Louise begin a correspondence and eventually marry, quite happily. Their marriage gets Justin out of Clove and back to her beloved South, but it also demonstrates that her mother, whom she has seen as weak, passive, and uninspired, can triumph in arenas where Ursula has known only failure.

The other enterprising thing in Louise's past is her elopement with Rivers Stokes. When her father writes the check for her first year's tuition at Sweet Briar, Louise offers to take the envelope to the mailbox. On the way she destroys the check and accomplishes two things: she remains "a devoted daughter" by saving them the tuition money at the same time she asserts herself as "a passionate, headstrong young woman" (*FS*, 32) by choosing to marry rather than to go to college.

Rivers Stokes is a man of great charm and little practicality, so the newly-weds move in with Louise's parents in order to prepare to face adult life. After Justin's birth, the grandparents rear the child so that Louise can go off to be a wife to Rivers, who is in college. This odd commingling of adulthood and childhood that characterizes the early years of her parents' marriage contributes to Justin's precocity and her feeling that she can somehow classify and thereby control the adults she encounters. Her memory of those years contributes to her diminished view of her mother to some extent. She thinks, "Leaving me feeling, almost as far back as I could remember, like a prematurely aged little parent myself, who must exercise self-restraint and empathy—the two chief virtues of my grandmother and grandfather, respectively—so that my mother could prolong her life as a girl" (*FS*, 40).

These stories of an enterprising young woman are fascinating to Justin because they provide a completely different version of her mother than the one she grows up with and nurtures while she sees herself as the "prematurely aged little parent." It is ironic that she overhears these stories when her mother is telling them to Becky. Becky seems as fascinated by Louise as Justin is by Ursula, and Justin feels envy and amazement that someone else can draw out of her mother things that are genuinely interesting, out of the ordinary.

Once she and her children arrive in Clove, of course, Louise must find new ways to be enterprising if her family is to survive. In trying to decide how to go forward with her life and to care adequately for Justin and Jem, Louise calls into question the years she spent as the protected wife and daughter whose parents assumed many of the responsibilities that should have been hers as an adult. When that questioning takes place and when her mother argues that Justin is probably better off for what Justin sees as inordinate suffering in her young life, because that suffering will make her better prepared to face adulthood with strength and independence, Justin is terribly shaken by the change in her mother. She sees it as irrevocably altering her sense of her childhood: "Her renouncement of the way she had been was ripping out some vital thread that had run through my whole childhood" (*FS*, 39).

At the same time Justin begins to feel uncomfortable with this new version of her mother, she finds what she considers her higher, more sensitive self reinforced and encouraged by Ursula. In her adolescent mind, that sets up a clear contrast, and her loyalties are temporarily assigned to Ursula. In order to maintain the negative feelings about her mother, whom she loves very much, the 14-year-old Justin must at times be intentionally cruel to Louise. Such cruelty to one's parent, especially to one's mother if the adolescent is a girl, is part of growing up and establishing a separate identity, of course. In Justin's case, the normal breaking away is exaggerated by the unusual circumstances of her childhood and her sudden dislocation and exacerbated by her meeting Ursula.

For example, Justin is well aware of her intentions during an argument with her mother: " 'You don't understand,' I said to my mother, wanting to hurt her as much as I could, 'because you don't understand *me*. I may be your daughter, but I've come to the sad conclusion that you don't understand the way my mind works or what is important to me. You just aren't capable of it' " (*FS*, 277). This intentionally cruel manipulation, although quite different in its motives, intensity, and consequences, echoes Ursula's treatment of her mother at the time she discovers her affair, and these echoes reinforce the fictive quality of the characters' lives.

Justin, however, ultimately chooses a different ending for her plot, and at 40 she is comfortable with the life her mother chooses with Craven Ravenel without feeling compelled to live a similar life herself. In that sense, she is, as an adult, very much the same as Cate and Lydia in *A Mother and Two Daughters* despite the Ursula-inspired high artistic nature of her profession.

The contrast between Ursula and Louise is not the only contrast that influences Justin's shifting image of her mother. Mona Mott is also a very different woman than her sister-in-law, and their differences influence Justin as well. Mona has chosen to separate from Eric Mott and to set herself on a course that eventually leads to an independent life. She is taking real estate courses and intends to be wealthy and to know something of the power that orphans seldom feel. When Justin and her family arrive in Clove, Mona is just beginning this process, and it takes a while for Justin to overcome her initial placement of Mona as someone firmly entrenched in the values represented by Lucas Meadows and IBM.

Mona is very proud of her home, so proud that she protects her beloved wall-to-wall carpeting with plastic runners. She has a strong sense of what a girl's room should be, so she decorates Justin's bedroom with shades of pink and curtains dominated by a repeated pattern of cheerful milkmaids. The sticky sweetness of this environment is a sore spot for Justin, and it takes gifts from Ursula—a faded poster from her brief sojourn in Europe as an aspiring actress and an unadorned blue bottle to create focus in the swirl of milkmaids happily pursuing their trade—to make her room bearable.

Justin also disagrees with Mona's pride in her home's being designed for the statistically typical family. There is, first of all, the irony of the family who actually lives there being so atypical.

Justin also sees the environment that Mona prides herself in as ironic, designed not for convenience but for conformity, the old Godwin nemesis, to which the residents then acquiesce, forfeiting any chance for the unordinary life. Yet, as she comes to know her aunt better, Justin begins to admire her "tenacious insistence on the truth" (*FS*, 31), which contrasts with both Ursula's creative manipulation of the facts and Louise's tendency to romanticize the past.

Mona succeeds in real estate, becomes fabulously wealthy, takes a gorgeous young lover, and lives a life Ursula DeVane would envy in Europe. The adult Justin considers Mona her friend and finds herself able to talk with her in ways that she can never talk with her mother. Mona's success provides Justin with one aspect of what she sought in Ursula as a role model. Mona lives a life outside the realm of the ordinary. Louise, whose brief stint as a martyr "determined to make suffering noble and beautiful" (*FS*, 35) bothered Justin, with her marriage to Craven, provides Justin with the other half of what Ursula was to have been—high romance. When her mother remarries, she restores for Justin the "glamorous, carefree" image that Justin held dear before their move (*FS*, 36). Because Justin herself attains the artistic life that rounded out what she expected to gain from Ursula, the novel ultimately provides everything Justin needs within the context of the family, and Ursula becomes inessential as anything more than the image necessary to stir up what already resides within Justin.

Although much of this resolution is not evident to Justin until years later, at 14 she is aware that her feelings for Ursula have been irrevocably altered and that she has somehow moved beyond her mentor and guide:

I did, truly, feel pity for her, for the wasted existence she was now doomed to, in that house filled with its terrible history. (With the romantic blindness of the young, it never occurred to me that she could leave the house, go somewhere else and start over. Something in me didn't even want it.) But the pity I felt for her left me free. I was glad not to be obsessed by her anymore. Glad not to be always wondering what she was doing, wondering if I felt "too much" for her: I felt like someone who had come in close contact with a fatal illness and survived—though others had not been so lucky. I hoped to get on with my own life, even if there were not many exciting prospects in this village. I frankly hoped to avoid meeting her. (*FS*, 307)

Once an ideal becomes an object of pity, it is impossible to maintain her in her elevated state. Inherent in pity is a sense of superiority, and with Justin's pity for Ursula comes a new appreciation of her own life and her abilities. She progresses from envying Ursula's life to realizing that she is better off with her own, especially since it includes her ability to imagine the other's life and the seemingly boundless potential of youth rather than the negotiated limits of middle age.

The Expansive Power of Sympathetic Art

The women in *A Mother and Two Daughters* all wonder at various times in that novel about the nature of power. Justin comes to understand very early that, for her, power will spring from precisely this talent for entering into the essence of another through her imagination. It will make her an artist. Her success in "becoming" Ursula leads to a satisfying feeling of accomplishment: "This feeling was accompanied by an agreeable surge of power. It was as if I had given myself an immunity from self-consciousness, through my exercise of impersonating Ursula DeVane" (*FS*, 110).

This crucial lesson is a turning point in Justin's life. It is also the critical connection between the resolution of *A Mother and Two Daughters* and this novel because it links to art the expansion of sympathies and the idea that power comes from relatedness portrayed in the epilogue to the earlier novel. Thus the struggle that has occupied Godwin's protagonists from the beginning of her career seems to have reached a positive and logical conclusion. The terrible self-consciousness that finally paralyzes her earliest protagonists and gives way to the limited progress in *The Odd Woman* and *Violet Clay* finds itself destroyed by the increasing engagement with others that marks *A Mother and Two Daughters* and *The Finishing School*.

With the victory that emerges in Justin's sorting out of the experiences of her fourteenth summer, Godwin reaches the end of the thematic idiom that has dominated her work for almost two decades. That opens up new possibilities for her, just as Justin's summer opens new possibilities. In a struggle that has meant so much to the characters Godwin has created and has been carried out with such intensity and such unwavering purpose, no victory comes without a feeling of nostalgia for the days of uncertainty and heady encounter. The victorious 40-year-old Justin suspects that she may, in her success, have moved beyond the sort of yearning that fueled her journey both toward and beyond Ursula DeVane. She speaks to her younger self in a plaintive tone that ironically seeks to rekindle those very feelings that she has worked toward controlling:

Oh, young Justin, what would I say to you if I could penetrate the time barrier and murmur in your ear? I am so much more certain of myself than you were; I am probably happier, as the world defines happiness. Yet, you draw me, you awaken me, as I watch you sitting there, surrounded by your treasures of so many intense desires and fears. Exult in your riches—though of course you won't—because the day will come when you will look back enviously on your longings. The day will come when you understand what Rilke was saying in that sonnet which Julian set to music: that the act of longing for something will always be more intense than the requiting of it. (*FS*, 211–12)

For the adult Justin, only her work can possess her as intensely as she was possessed during her summer with Ursula. To be so possessed by one's work is, of course, what Violet, Cate, and Lydia all strive toward; the lack of that possession is what keeps Dane and Francesca from victory. "Most of the time," the older Justin thinks, "I consider this a victory. Sometimes, however, it makes me a little sad" (*FS*, 322).

Mature vision is the compensation for this sadness at losing youth's capacity for longing and self. The Justin who survives and looks back at her youth realizes what mature vision means: "I've reached the point in my life when I can see it from everybody's side. I can understand why every one of us behaved the way we did, and probably couldn't have behaved any other way" (*FS*, 169). In *A Southern Family,* her next novel, Godwin uses that same kind of vision to write her first novel that combines the first-person narration of *The Finishing School* with the multiple points of view of *A Mother and Two Daughters*. Set in the same city as *The Odd Woman* and *A Mother and Two Daughters* and featuring an accomplished artist, in the tradition of Violet Clay and Justin Stokes, this time a writer, *A Southern Family* is Godwin's debut of a new rhetoric of fiction, one firmly founded on the substantial work that precedes it and so thoroughly and skillfully progresses to the definitive statements of her original idiom that *A Mother and Two Daughters* and *The Finishing School* represent.

Chapter Five
Seeing It from Everybody's Side: A Southern Family

Several qualities of *A Southern Family* make it a departure from Godwin's previous novels. For the first time, she uses multiple points of view, several of them rendered in the first person. The closest she comes to this narrative strategy in the earlier novels is the alternating chapters from Cameron and Francesca Bolt's perspectives in *Glass People* and the old-fashioned omniscience of *A Mother and Two Daughters,* in which her narrator is obviously more interested in Nell, Cate, and Lydia than in any of the other characters. In *A Southern Family* the narrative interest is spread across a much broader spectrum: it includes male characters, characters from a variety of social classes, characters with varying degrees of connection to the central action. There is no pretense of omniscience; the narrative in each section is limited, quite tightly, to one or sometimes two perspectives.

In *A Mother and Two Daughters* when Cate and a friend discuss the concept of the "worst" sin, her friend feels that it is denying someone his or her own nature, making a person feel inferior or ashamed of the essential self. Although much is wide and generous in her previous work, Godwin's preoccupation with women who have a particular and narrowly defined essential self is, in part, a failure to acknowledge other natures, other selves. Nowhere in her earlier work does Godwin attain such wholehearted respect for a spectrum of essential selves as she manages in *A Southern Family* because of the multiple perspectives. Her narrative technique allows all the characters the dignity of their own natures.

Another departure is that, for the first time in a novel, Godwin creates a protagonist who shares her profession. One of the central figures of the story is Clare Campion, the eldest child of the family to which the title refers and a famous novelist. Although earlier protagonists such as Jane Clifford and Cate Galitsky, who are literature professors, Violet Clay, a painter, and Justin Stokes, an actress, embody what are clearly aspects of their creator's professional life, Clare's being a novelist allows Godwin the opportunity to establish her own theories of fiction as an artform that the earlier artists and literary figures did not.

Another significant difference in *A Southern Family* and the earlier work is that the typical Godwin heroine—in this novel represented by Clare Campion—is now (and now sees herself as) a secondary character. This shift is in part a result of the use of multiple perspectives and is another indication of the author's acknowledgment of others' natures, their essential selves. No longer is the main story to be told that of a sensitive, independent young woman seeking her best life. That young woman is still here, obviously older, but still seeking the best life. The crucial difference is that the swirl of events and characters that surrounds her is too complex, too insistent and demanding, to allow her the luxury of concentrating quite so intently on the personal as the Godwin woman has been able to do previously.

As *A Southern Family* opens up new directions in Godwin's work, however, it also provides a clear culmination of other strands that have been woven throughout her body of fiction. The novel's title makes clear that this is the story of a family, particularly a southern one, and certainly that theme has evolved into one of Godwin's primary concerns. Although the birth family is not so directly important in *The Perfectionists,* beginning with *Glass People* and growing more and more important in the subsequent novels, the places and the people from which Godwin's main characters have come have been key elements in defining the characters and their plots.

In these earlier novels, though, the theme of family has served as a backdrop for other themes that could be labeled primary, and the action in those stories that relates directly to the family situation is most often secondary action. In *A Southern Family, the* central concern is family. Once the interest shifts from the individual to the group, the necessity for greater narrative complexity is unavoidable, and the expansion of scope and thematic concern also seems inevitable.

Another important theme developed throughout Godwin's career is the tendency of her characters, especially her female characters, to see their lives as performances, themselves as actors in a drama partly of their own making, partly a by-product of their environment and conditioning. In *A Southern Family* this theme also finds its fullest expression. The single action of one family member, Theo Quick, causes everyone else to examine his or her part in Quick family drama, causes each individual whose consciousness the novel explores to evaluate the role he or she plays in the unfolding of events before and after the momentary act that calls the foundations of family life into question. In addition to generating the story this novel tells, this profound examination of self-as-actor that takes place in *A Southern Family,* read with full knowledge of the work that precedes it, is, in a sense, a reexamination of the author's body of work as well.

Thus, drawing conclusions about *A Southern Family* is a way of also drawing conclusions about Godwin as novelist. Thinking about the questions raised by the novel, not the least of them the connection between autobiographical events and the events that unfold in the novel, is an excellent way to consider the author's career as she enters her third decade as a writer.

You Can Go Home Again—Till It Breaks Wide Open

A Southern Family opens with a familiar scene in Godwin's canon: an expatriate southerner has returned home for a visit. Here the expatriate is Clare Campion, home to Mountain City, North Carolina, for a birthday visit to her mother, Lily Quick. It is October, the most beautiful season in the Blue Ridge, and the first two sections of the novel suggest that this story will focus on issues that Godwin's readers will quickly recognize.

The first section is from the point of view of Julia Richardson, Clare's best friend from childhood and the closest Mountain City comes to providing her with a soulmate. Clare has made fiction of Julia's life in one of her novels, *The Headmaster's Daughters.* (If readers wish at this point to begin making connections between Godwin's body of fiction and Clare's, noting that Mountain City is also the setting for Godwin's novel *A Mother and Two Daughters,* as well as the unnamed setting for *The Odd Woman,* and that Julia is a resident of Mountain City, it is safe to assume that *The Headmaster's Daughters* is to Clare what *A Mother and Two Daughters* is to Godwin.) This choice of Julia as the opening perspective for the novel signals that the family of the title will be observed from outside, something not typical for Godwin's main characters. In addition Julia provides a necessary objectivity at the same time she is close enough to the family to allow true intimacy, both crucial to establishing a foundation from which the reader may enter the chaos that is shortly to erupt.

In the second section of the novel, entitled "Olympians," Julia and Clare take a day from Clare's visit for themselves to picnic atop a mountain. There they have the standard perspective for typical Godwin women, in that they feel elevated, superior, to most of what lies below them. They discuss the Quicks, Mountain City, their past and present, together and apart, all without any real attention to the essence of others. They are bright, attractive, appealing women, and their conversation does not make them seem narrow or self-absorbed in any way. It is, in fact, a perfectly natural sort of conversation for two old friends to have. The scene, the characters, the conversation are known quantities for Godwin readers. In fact, if the entire novel were to be devoted to these women and the issues their conversation raises, the book would probably be redundant.

But what Godwin is about here is a painstaking narrative manipulation that positions her readers with her characters—on familiar territory, thinking "OK, I know these people, I know the sort of things that are probably going to happen to them. I know at least the range of possibilities for what can happen to them."

The challenge to known territory, to the sense that one is operating with a clearly charted map of Godwin country, is connected in these opening sections to the writing of fiction through Theo Quick's probing at what he sees as a weakness in his half-sister as a writer. He says to her on the evening of their mother's birthday celebration, "Why don't you write a book about something that can *never* be wrapped up? . . . What if you came across something like that in life? Would you want to write about it?"[1] Clare's answer is that she would write about such a thing only if it interested her but that she usually does not find that the "unwrappable chaos and meaninglessness and dreariness that goes on the world" (*ASF,* 91–92) excites her curiosity. It is not the stuff of Campion fiction.

If one again extrapolates from Campion to Godwin, then the assumption is that the challenge to Campion's fiction is also a challenge to Godwin's fiction and that her alter ego's response that the unwrappable is not inherently curious or interesting to her is not unlike the response Clare Campion's creator might make to a similar inquiry.

The day after the birthday celebration, the same afternoon that Julia and Clare enjoy from their Olympian perch atop the mountain, Theo Quick dies a violent and mysterious death. The police ruling is that he murdered his lover while her child looked on, then turned the gun on himself and commited suicide. At the level of plot, of course, Theo's action disrupts the normal, charted territory of family life and sets those he leaves behind on a search for answers and new direction. The novel covers the year after his death, and the focus shifts from his mother and father to his siblings and his ex-wife and also maintains some of the objectivity established by opening the novel with Julia Richardson's point of view through using her and Sister Patrick, a nun who has been close to the family for many years, as additional observers of the events of that year.

The world in which Godwin's characters have lived up until the moment Theo dies is not a world that includes the sort of random violence, the chaos, of that event. A main character's worst brush with crime in the earlier novels is the Enema Bandit of *The Odd Woman,* a character kept offstage and used primarily in a symbolic way, often for comic relief. There have been suicides in the earlier novels, most notably those of Ambrose Clay and Julian DeVane, but those suicides are, to a certain extent, understandable, even predictable, according to the terms those novels establish.

In *A Southern Family* Theo's death and the murky circumstances that surround it truly shatter the Godwin world as it has been previously defined. His is not the precise, thoughtful suicide of Ambrose Clay; it is not the desperate act of a man shattered by sudden discovery of unbearable truth, as is the case with Julian DeVane. The act is messy and incomprehensible from the moment it happens until the next year; there are missing pieces and details that will never come clear. It is precisely the sort of event that Theo describes to his sister as the stuff of better fiction than she has written to date: it is something that can never be wrapped up.

Thus, the main impetus for the novel's plot also becomes an impetus for a new kind of Godwin fiction. The manner of the story's telling—the multiple perspectives—is necessary because the story cannot be wrapped up from a single perspective, even from a number of perspectives. The essential perspective is missing, dead, before the question is raised, and everyone left behind must struggle to come to his or her own answers without adequate information. The complexity of the novel comes, in part, from the unsolvable nature of its essential mystery, but it also springs from the interaction, sometimes the collision, of the different survivors' efforts to assemble the "truth" that they each individually need.

As Cate comes to her sense of recognition and reconciliation in *A Mother and Two Daughters,* as the story heads toward a neatly wrapped ending, Theo might say, she has an insight into her mother as a woman with private stories that would explain the person that the daughter has come to know. Cate wonders why it is that one's family and the relationships that exist within that most fundamental of groups can be penetrated and understood only in hindsight. (Her conclusion that such penetration and understanding are, finally, possible, blessed with the luxury of hindsight, is certainly reaffirmed by *The Finishing School* and Godwin's decision to have a 40-year-old Justin Stokes narrate a story about the events of her fourteenth summer. In this case, hindsight is the basis of the entire narrative strategy.)

A Southern Family sets itself a much harder problem with which to wrestle, for hindsight does not work here. There is some penetration of the mysteries of family life that lead both to "normal" attitudes and relationships, as defined within the unique family structure being examined, and to tragedy. But understanding and a tightly wrapped ending prove impossible in the face of Theo's challenge, which is two-edged here. There is the challenge of his death itself and how the family will endure that event, and there is the challenge to Clare as a writer: how will she deal with his death in her work, if she chooses to confront this story that cannot be finished in the way she would normally resolve conflict?

The intricacies about family life and about fiction writing that *A Southern Family* confronts are made more unwieldy by the autobiographical elements of the story. Godwin's half-brother did die a violent death, similar to the one portrayed in the novel, and many of the unanswerable questions raised by the novel remain unanswered for the real incident from which the story springs. Godwin has expressed her feelings about the uses of autobiography in fiction writing in several essays, concluding, as do most writers who venture their thoughts on the subject, that the lines between reality and fiction are always and forever too murky, finally, to be drawn convincingly. It is best to read and to analyze *A Southern Family* on its own terms, as fiction, knowing only that the added element of autobiographical connection is but another example of what the novel comes to say about what we can and cannot know to be the "truth."

Coming to Terms with Limits in Fiction and in Life

Late in the novel, as Julia drives Clare to Columbia, South Carolina, after an oddly disturbing and amusing visit with the Mullins clan, the family of Theo's ex-wife, Clare tells Julia that Theo's question about her fiction has been instructive to her, even though she suspects that Theo had never actually read any of her books. She says, "I haven't decided whether it's more a flaw or a shortcoming, but, whichever, it limits my writing. I won't let things be themselves. I arrange things around me the way I want them . . . the way I need them to be . . . and shut the rest out. . . . it may also be too late for me to train myself to see things as they are . . . even when they're ambiguous or just disappointingly dull . . . compared with how I imagined it would be beforehand" (*ASF,* 371–72).

Julia suggests that Clare is confusing her guilt about her shortcomings as a sister with her work. "Art *is*," Julia reminds her, "moving things around" (*ASF,* 372). To separate the two, Julia advises her friend to answer a letter that Theo had written to Clare a decade earlier, in which he asks her to respond, when she has time, with a letter describing a typical day in her life. Her letter, written some months after Theo's death, becomes a chapter of the novel. In it Clare struggles to define what fiction has meant to her and what it will mean, now that she has had to confront both Theo's death and his challenge to her work.

She begins by telling Theo about two books that she has been reading, or trying to read. Although not mentioned by name, the novels are, as Godwin's descriptions of them make clear, *Edisto,* by Padgett Powell, and *The Unbearable Lightness of Being,* by Milan Kundera. Although Clare has been looking forward to reading both, she confides in Theo that they have disappointed her. She is put off by their "show-offy, peacockish tone," of which she finds male writers often guilty (*ASF,* 377), and she is even more disappointed in Kundera's attitude toward his characters. She says to Theo about that author's announcement that he needn't even try to persuade readers of his characters' "reality":

Well, then, why go to the trouble of writing about them? . . . The answer, of course, is that he needed them, needed their flatness, the lack of crucial information we are given about them, in order to display to best advantage his own contrasting flesh-and-blood roundness, his greater historical reality. The pleasure to be got from such a book has little to do with your feelings or curiosity about the stick-figure characters being manipulated by the author, and everything to do with how far you are willing, or able, to admire the mind of the manipulator. (*ASF,* 377)

Clare then goes on in her letter to compare the main incident of Kundera's book—the invasion of the narrator's hometown by Russian tanks—with the main event of Powell's—the main character's discovery that his mother is having an affair with a man he considers unsuitable for her—and questions whether the event of overwhelming social consequence, the invasion, is necessarily more important than the event of more personal consequence, the young man's discovery of "something painful about [his] mother" (*ASF,* 378). Clare concludes,

Both were the incidents the respective narrators had felt most deeply as the betrayals that changed their lives. Yet many people I know, if asked publicly (publicly may be the key word here) which was the more "serious" incident, would answer dutifully, "Oh, the Russian tanks. The other is just, well, after all, one adolescent boy's feelings about his mother." Then I imagined what I would say if I were put on the spot, publicly, and I am happy to report to you that I amazed everyone present, from the editors of *The New York Times* to Ivy League Distinguished Professors to big shots in the Reagan administration, with my perspicacity by replying calmly, "How long will it take us to see the connection between the occurrence of wars and the way parents treat their children?" (An idea stolen from a book by a woman psychoanalyst I recently was reading in an effort to find clues to *you.*) (*ASF,* 378)

Clearly, her opening this very personal letter by discussing her attitudes toward contemporary fiction ties into the confusion about her role as sister and her role as novelist that Julia points out in their discussion in the preceding chapter. That Clare finds her imagined dazzling answer about the "burning" issues of the current literary scene in a nonfiction psychology book she is examining for information about her dead brother intertwines the fact and the fiction, the theory and the reality, even more. It also strengthens the connection between Theo and Clare's ongoing "joint" examination of her own fiction.

In her letter Clare moves from commenting on the fiction of these two males whose novels she did not particularly like to explaining to her brother her reasons for moving to her current rural New York home. She came to the place from which she writes him in the same summer that he sent her the letter asking for a response detailing a day in her life. Obviously, her life now, as an accomplished and rewarded novelist, is different from the life she led a decade earlier, when she came to this house as a last effort to write the kind of fiction she wanted to write: "deep-breathing, reflective, and with that patience for detail I admired in those medieval stone carvers who would lavish their skills on the lowliest gargoyle simply because . . . that was their job for the day, and every day's work was done for the glory of God . . . [not] shallow gulps of prose, fragmented narratives peopled with unfinished beings whose creator was too tired, or too demoralized to imagine them in loving detail" (*ASF,* 380–81).

This description of the fiction Clare set as her goal is, in fact, a fair assessment of the kind of fiction Godwin herself has written. As her character goes on explaining her success to her brother, however, Clare becomes aware of her tone and of how it would strike her brother. She says, "The tone makes me recoil, too. It embarrasses me, just as the unexpected richness of my present life embarrasses me, especially since you made me aware of it in the kitchen last October" (*ASF,* 381). Having acknowledged this embarrassment, Clare goes on to retell that story with self-conscious awareness of the impact of tone, while also acknowledging that Theo perhaps was passing judgment on her life as well as her work.

What happens in this extended analysis of herself, her work, and Theo's commentary on that self and that work is that Clare comes to articulate a description of how the writer's mind works that meshes quite well with the impression of the artistic mind at work created by Godwin's fiction itself. After a long account of the profundity of Theo's comments on that October afternoon, Clare admits that the profundity is the result of her "dissembling after the fact" (*ASF,* 383), which, she admits, she has also done in her description of her carefully thought-out move to the country.

These inextricable links between fact and dissimulation are the basis of most of Godwin's comments on the role of autobiography in fiction; anyone who reads those essays will be aware that the final layer of dissimulation, that last mask hiding the essential self, may never be removed. In this passage, and in this significantly different novel as a whole, the author comes closer to exposing the true surface of those essential selves in her characters than she has ever done before. After making her admissions to Theo, Clare comes back to the analysis of Kundera that began her thoughts on fiction in the first place. She tells Theo that her "carefully constructed endorsement of 'full' writing" had been arranged only that morning, as she wanted to explain herself to him and, at the same time, defend herself against the presence of the "Russian-tank man" on the literary scene. Behind the dissimulation she first presents lies something closer to her true self: "I saw an opportunity to heroinize myself in retrospect and, at the same time, discreetly 'puff' my own methods—what I have learned I do best—at the expense of his and some enemies'/rivals' styles" (*ASF,* 383).

A little later in this letter to her dead brother, Clare describes the novel she was working on and was "fairly pleased" with at the time of his death. That novel, which was to have featured three "*major male characters,*" was to have broken new ground in Clare's career: "It was going to *get beyond* family life and the South and independent young-ish women wriggling out of the deadly twin-embrace" (*ASF,* 384). But when she returns to New York after Theo's funeral, Clare can no longer feel pleasure in that novel or respect the work she has done. In fact, she experiences "total revulsion" when she rereads what she has written and questions her original motives: "Whom, for God's sake, had I been trying to impress . . . or fool? Towards what crass marketplace had I been trundling my spurious wares, while maintaining a deceptive Jamesian slow-march of prose to keep the critics from thinking I had 'gone commercial'?" (*ASF,* 385).

For Clare the recognition of that rereading is a confrontation with her own tendency to dissimulate, to mask the essential self, in which she cannot stop believing. She tells Theo that "Confronting that material . . . was like catching an unexpected glimpse of myself in the mirror and seeing the outlines of a person for whom I—the genuine 'I,' if there is such a thing; yes, damn my nervous curtsy to fashionable theories, I still believe there exists a bedrock reality of the self—felt contempt" (*ASF,* 385).

Clare's ultimate solution—worked out on a family beach vacation the summer after Theo's death—is to begin another novel; its first chapters are about old friends going on a mountain picnic during a glorious fall, as the opening chapters of *A Southern Family* are about this same thing. Thus, the threads of fiction and reality are woven tighter. The book Clare Campion writes after her half-brother dies violently is virtually the same book Gail Godwin writes after her half-brother dies violently.

The Amateur Storyteller and the Art of Survival

Not everyone in the Quick family is a writer. Not everyone can deal with grief by transforming reality into fiction. Nor can the making of the fiction in this case tie up the loose ends or answer the unanswerable questions, as the old Clare and the old Godwin might have. *A Southern Family* ends as Clare begins her novel; the tying up is, of necessity, left undone. Another function of the way *A Southern Family* is told is that Clare, the writer, is certainly not the only storyteller in the novel. Indeed, part of the southernness of this novel is the way that storytelling permeates it, winds itself through every crack and crevice and attempts to fill in the blanks that reality can never close.

The most vivid representations of the southern tradition of storytelling in the novel are the Gallants, Alicia and Anthony. Dr. Anthony, now dead, is both storyteller and the stuff of others' stories. His sister, Alicia, is Ralph Quick's best friend and comforter. When he cannot get along with his wife, which is most of the time, he turns to Miss Alicia, who is in her late eighties, for companionship and solace. The Gallants, who have always lived on the same street where Julia Richardson grew up and now visits her retired father, are of the very highest echelon of old southern society: graceful and genteel and arrogant. Ralph—who was born to a much lower station in life, married above himself, and finally worked hard and earned enough money to find himself within reach of these people once so unattainable to him and his kind—is, by clinging to Miss Alicia, clinging to a past that is already over without his having experienced it as he longs to do.

The stories of the genteel class, those that attract Ralph and sustain the likes of the Gallants, are the basis of a whole southern mythos that has repelled and bound Godwin characters almost from the beginning of her career. The shifting nature of the region and its stories is the source of speculation on Clare's part about how those stories shape or failed to shape those they held sway over. She thinks:

An era had died with the passing of Dr. Anthony and his kind—the last generation to believe in their stories and feel no modern self-consciousness or guilt about the reasons for all those self-serving myths and legends, the highly embroidered tapestry of the sacred Old Locale. Many people would say such an era was better off dead. Clare herself thought so, up to a point. She had learned to see the flaws in the fabric. She knew perfectly well that her fate would not have been a happy one if she had been born into the heyday of the society Dr. Anthony loved to describe: a society distrustful of new ideas and strangers, where archaic customs were respected more than living accomplishments, and mediocrity often hid behind grace and style. . . . conversely, Clare often wondered if she would have developed into quite a different person—or, rather, failed to develop—if she had been born into one of those families whose belief in the divine right of their clan exempted her from having to strive for anything more. (*ASF,* 416–17)

The problem with the kind of stories Anthony Gallant represents is that they prevent the sort of transformation that takes place in the closing chapters and the epilogue of *A Mother and Two Daughters,* where the threatened Old Guard is fluid enough to make room for the strange new twists that pop up in the plots they thought they had controlled. In this sense, the stories that die with the passing of Dr. Anthony's generation are not art according to the definition Clare's lover Felix gives for art. He says, "An artist has found his true subject, I think, when he dramatizes the truth he can no longer escape rather than the illusions he has been longing to make true" (*ASF,* 461). (Felix's comment on art is based on a comment on *Wuthering Heights* made by Thomas Moser and recorded in Godwin's journal in December of 1975 ["Keeping," 82]. That the author incorporates something from a journal that is a decade old in a novel about an author who is seriously reexamining her work indicates how deep Godwin's own reexamination took her into her literary and personal past.)

This distinction between true art, true subject matter, and a false or lesser art that strives to preserve illusions, however dependent the creator may be on those illusions, is, of course, what Clare is working toward in her long letter to Theo. It is also the distinction that rests at the heart of the Quicks' reactions to Theo's death. Ralph, Lily, Rafe, and Clare tell themselves stories about what happened, and the stories come to represent how close each teller can come to inescapable truth—how far he or she can move from illusions.

Snow Mullins, Theo's ex-wife and the mother of his son, Jason, is as far from Dr. Anthony Gallant on the social spectrum as a white southerner can get. The stories of her class and her childhood are necessarily different from those the Gallants grew up with and have clung to with tenacity for almost a century. Snow is also a far cry from the intellectual richness of Felix Rohr's life. But she too has a commentary to make on the role of storytelling, of artifice, as it relates to the Quicks. In the section of the novel from Snow's point of view, Godwin has her most uneducated character call into question precisely the modus operandi that has been the hallmark of her characters throughout her career. Snow says of Clare and the other Quicks:

I could just hear her. And I've heard her enough times since to know I'm right. Turning everything into a little story that suits herself. In this case, looking down on us, but at the same time making it all right with her friends, turning it to her advantage that we was so quaint and old and "romantic." It didn't make a bit of difference what the truth was, why Theo really married me, why I married him. Clare is just like the rest of them in that respect. No, she's worse. Because she makes up lies about real people and writes them down in books and makes lots of money off the lies. She wrote that big, long book about her best and oldest friend, and I heard the Queen Mother [Lily] laugh once and say she had actually forgot Julia's father's real name at some Library Board meeting. She had called him by the name of the character in the book instead. "But he didn't mind," she said. "He laughed, too. I think he was rather pleased."
Another story. Who knows how pleased he really was? (*ASF,* 241)

Of all the Quicks, Clare is, of course, the most aware of the family tendency to "write" the convenient story and create the artifact that best preserves the necessary illusion. Quite early in the novel—almost as soon as she learns of her brother's death and the circumstances, known and unknown, that surround it—she says to Julia about the family's manner of dealing with the tragedy, "Each of us will take what we know about Theo and create our own speculations, and, knowing this family, each theory will serve that family member's particular, necessary myth" (*ASF,* 95). Much later in the novel, after Julia and Clare have spent an odd Sunday afternoon at the table of the Mullins family in Granny Squirrel, their native ground, Clare is still trying to figure out what happened and to formulate the speculation that will work for her. As the details, assumptions, and conclusions swirl around her brain and as she tries to sort them out on the drive away from the Mullinses and Granny Squirrel by talking with Julia, her friend realizes that at some point, when Quicks are the subject, the interpretative aspect of storytelling fails. "Maybe," Julia thinks, "in some cases narrative was as far as you could go" (*ASF,* 369).

The storyteller's inability, in certain instances, to interpret is an important lesson for the Quicks to learn as they try to deal with Theo's death. Eventually, the version that each Quick accepts will have to remain narrative laced with speculation. Logical, reasonable interpretation will remain forever impossible in this case. This same lesson, the limitations of a storyteller's interpretative powers, is also part of the theory of fiction being worked out by Godwin and by Clare Campion. As storytellers, one real and one her fictional creation, Godwin and Clare must accept the limitations that Julia acknowledges as she listens to her friend try to sort out the events the novel deals with.

If one must accept a limited ability to interpret, that suggests that perhaps the essence of storytelling becomes simpler, a matter of narrating observable facts and reporting the truth. There is nothing straightforward about the stories or the tellers in *A Southern Family*, however. As Theo says to Felix the summer before his death, "What's sad about our family, and why we're probably doomed, is that we haven't been able to be ourselves. Everyone of us has wasted too much time being ashamed of the wrong things" (*ASF,* 300). Theo is expressing a trait common to characters throughout Godwin's career in that he is blaming the tendency to play roles, to create selves that hide the essential self, for the unhappiness of his family. However, the characters in the earlier work, even those who do possess an ironic awareness of the manner in which they conduct their lives, often stop well short of Theo's acknowledgment of the negative impact of this approach to life.

Twice in the novel, Snow Mullins echoes Theo's observation. On the first occasion, she is discussing the Quicks' inability to speak the truth. She says, "The truth is what suits *them,* they have no respect for anything else" (*ASF,* 216), and later she adds, "it's like they are all acting in a play or something. Each one's got themself a part, and they have to stay in that part as long as they're around the others" (*ASF,* 236). Although Snow is an unlikely source of wisdom, her conclusions about the Quicks are very similar to Clare's, and even as Clare shares her mother's and the other Quicks' negative view of Snow, she finds herself drawn to her sister-in-law's access to elements of the truth and pieces of the story they are all trying to tell that none of the others have.

Finally, *A Southern Family* suggests that modern southerners, those who follow the generation represented by the Gallants, fall into two categories. Stripped of their innocent, unself-conscious acceptance of the stories that rearrange truth to make life comfortable, the contemporary southerner, ironic and self-aware, must come to terms with the stories and how they will or will not be used to keep individual lives afloat. The majority—in the novel everyone except Theo—negotiate some compromise within themselves, arrange things—truth and story—in whatever proportions allow them to move forward in the direction they want to go. Some, represented in the novel by Theo, are unable to adopt the ironic stance necessary to continue the lives they have been brought up to live.

On the first evening of the novel, the night of Lily's birthday celebration, Theo and Jason walk Julia to her car as she is leaving. During college, Theo was a student in one of her history classes, and he has always made Julia feel slightly uncomfortable. Because he dropped her class, there is between them a feeling of unfinished business. On this evening before his death, he challenges Julia about what meaning there is in life. Their exchange serves to establish the difference in the two routes available to the postmodern southerner. Julia says:

"Trying to understand excites me." But the words rushed out too quickly, and though true—perhaps her truest—sounded cheap.

"To understand what?" [Theo] pressed.

"Everything," she said impatiently, frustrated at herself for not being more eloquent, at him for wanting too much from her. "All the patterns and the meanings. The mysteries of people. How it all adds up."

She knew exactly what he would answer, and he did. "What if it doesn't add up to anything? What if there are no patterns or meanings? What if there's nothing to understand?" (*ASF,* 41)

Julia is expressing the same belief in essential truth, essential self, essential meaning that Clare expresses in her letter to Theo when she withdraws her self-conscious bow to fashionable skepticism and says outright that she does believe in a true, essential self. Theo's fear that no such self or truth exists is, as Julia indicates, a predictable response, sophomoric even, if one wants to read their encounter in terms of their teacher-student relationship. It is straight out of Existentialism 101. Another way of interpreting Theo's conclusion is to read it as an outgrowth of the inescapable hold of storytelling, role playing, and myth making on his family and his culture. Theo may have concluded that this hold is so strong, so pervasive that the way to whatever truth and pattern may have once existed for human beings has been forever obscured.

Thus, his marriage to Snow can be read as an effort to leap backward in time, in society's development, to find a way of life that is not hopelessly layered in stories and posturing. Snow says of their relationship, "at least I done him the courtesy of seeing who he really was and not what they wanted to make him into or keep him from being. Not that *who he really was* was all that easy to see. Most of the time he was covering it up one way and another . . . trying so hard to be what they wanted" (*ASF,* 235). Obviously, whatever efforts Snow and Theo make, they are not able to overcome the way of life that the Quick family represents. The effort to be oneself, separate from the context of family and society, is, for Theo, a doomed effort, which, perhaps, explains the goal he announces to Julia during their talk the night before he dies. He says to her, "I'll tell you something that excites me. The idea of all this being over. Of me, as far away as those stars, looking down on it and not feeling involved anymore" (*ASF*, 40–41).

For Theo, the only way to escape Quick-ness (with the family name's obvious connection to life-ness) is death. Snow's conclusion that Theo's family "took away his natural joy in himself" (*ASF*, 236) again recalls the discussion about sin between Cate and her friend in *A Mother and Two Daughters*. Snow suggests that the Quicks denied Theo his essential self, made him dislike and deny his nature, which, for Cate's friend, was the worst of all sins against the Holy Ghost. Snow's sense that Theo was, in fact, trying to be something other than his true self in order to satisfy the demands of his family also recalls *The Scarlet Letter*, which figures so prominently in *A Mother and Two Daughters*, and Arthur Dimmesdale's effort to wear one face to the world and another to himself. Hawthorne warns that the man who attempts this dual nature for very long soon forgets which is the true self and becomes hopelessly and forever confused.

Dealing with the Deadly Twin Embrace

If Theo is a character in this tradition and if his dilemma is grounded in his being a member of a particular southern family that represents the tendencies of a particular culture, then he becomes an archetype for one of the themes that has dominated Godwin's work from the beginning. Clare recalls her comment to Theo in her letter that the book she was working on at the time of his death was to have gotten beyond the issue of "independent young-ish women wriggling out of the deadly twin-embrace" of "family life and the South" (*ASF*, 384), but she abandons that book and eventually begins a book that opens much as *A Southern Family* does. Theo and his death thus become Godwin's most fundamental confrontation with the very issues that her alter ego, Clare as novelist, was trying to move beyond or avoid.

In this sense, then, *A Southern Family* is two stories: a traditional plot—a young man dies a violent and mysterious death, his survivors try to comprehend then move forward—and the author's reexamination of the novel form as she has practiced it. For the second of these stories, *A Southern Family* suggests that Godwin, like Clare Campion, was not ready to move beyond the story of characters trying to escape that deadly twin-embrace of family and region. Although the novel does finally seem to grant Theo the right to *his* decision about that necessary escape, it does not put forward that decision as the only, or the best, option.

One healthy consequence of Theo's death is that all those close to him, especially his family, must rethink their accommodations to those twins of family and region that hold them all, even Clare, tighter than they might have admitted before the death shatters illusions they have clung to for many years. More than anyone, Lily Quick can be seen as the source of the story the Quicks have been telling themselves for as long as they can remember. It is Lily's vision of family and culture that shapes all the Quicks. Even Snow, who resists quite fiercely the identity the Queen Mother tries to impose on her once Lily realizes she cannot stop Theo's marriage, internalizes everything Lily stands for and expects of others. Snow does not practice these things, for Lily's approval is not important to her, but as soon as it becomes convenient for her own purposes and to attain her personal goals, Snow demonstrates that not a moment of Lily's shaping of an ideal Snow has been wasted.

During the hearing that determines whether Snow or Ralph and Lily will have custody of Jason following Theo's death, Snow appears to testify wearing the proper lady-like suit her former mother-in-law selected for her during her marriage. She answers the questions posed to her while she is testifying in the King's English that Lily has tried to drill into her. She plays the role she had refused to play when Lily wanted her to in order to defeat Lily in court and regain custody of her son. To the extent that Snow has to play a role that contradicts her essential self, even though she regains her son, she also loses because she cannot win her son *and* maintain the integrity of the self she is without Lily's manipulation. Snow must make certain compromises that Theo was finally unable to make, must be able to maintain the separate selves required to negotiate the treacherous waters of southern family life, in order to win Jason. She must play Lily's game in order to defeat Lily, but the necessity of the game indicates that the victory is not without its costs and therefore can never be a complete triumph.

Lily is famous for driving around Mountain City with her gas tank on empty. This bad habit is partly the result of the contemporary preponderance of pump-it-yourself stations; Lily is obviously not a pump-it-yourself woman. The habit is also a metaphor for the way of life Lily represents. Her sense of family and culture—of the best life, to use the phrase so many of Godwin's female characters use—is running on empty, too. In one of the novel's key scenes involving Lily, she finds herself out of gas and walking up the long hill to her home. On that walk she has a vision of sainthood, of what it would be like to transcend herself, and in this vision even Lily, the master of the life story that cripples Theo and perplexes even her daughter, the writer and perhaps her greatest admirer, recognizes what her children and others also come to know during the course of the novel.

As she climbs toward her fractured home, Lily realizes,

> If she could make it to the top of the hill carrying her entire and acknowledged load of sorrows and mistakes, as well as all the evils experience had taught her human beings were capable of visiting on one another, it seemed to her she might be granted a kind of spiritual second wind. . . . And somewhere during the ultimate stretch of this honest walk home, after years of "running on empty" inside a protective vehicle, she would be shown how to divest herself of personal grievances (ranging from broken soap dishes to malicious daughters-in-law): how to die to herself without actually dying. What a refreshing atmosphere to live in! (*ASF*, 212)

The key word in this passage is perhaps *honest;* its being a part of Lily's thought process indicates that she is fully aware of the dishonest nature of much of her existence. In many ways, Lily is the most spiritual character in the novel, with the exception of the priests and Sister Patrick, but she has, to a large extent, kept her spiritual life, her pursuit of a higher truth, separate from her real life, from her relationships with others, even those closest to her—her husband and her children.

Lily is stopped short in her metaphorical journey toward a transcendent self when Ralph and Jason come along to give her a ride home just before she has a chance to accomplish the task she has set herself for the completed journey. She gets into the car with them and thus sacrifices the chance to know whether her vision of a new, better self would have been realized. In the novel's final chapter, told alternately from Lily's point of view and from the point of view of Sister Patrick, the nun who has known the Quick family for many years and who has been involved in the educations of the Quick children, Lily is again traveling, but this time Sister Patrick is with her. The occasion is the first anniversary of Theo's death, and the two women make another uphill journey, to the site of a mountaintop chapel where Sister Patrick has been on retreat.

In their conversation during the drive to the chapel, Sister Patrick asks Lily about her habit of visiting older people in nursing homes in the city. Lily says she began the visits as an expression of thanks that her own mother had not withered slowly in a way that would have been a terrible affront to her mother's dignity. Gradually, Lily tells the nun, she has come to feel enormous anger at the way old people are treated by our society. She says, "Every one of them is a unique personality, even though their bodies are in the process of crumbling to dust. Everybody's body crumbles to dust eventually, but no two personalities—*no two*—are ever alike" (*ASF,* 525). Sister Patrick agrees, saying, "I'm like you. I believe the personality is important. Otherwise, why did God make everyone unique? And since He did, we should fight any person or institution or system that tries to take away that dignity of uniqueness" (*ASF,* 525). Behind this exchange, coming as it does at the novel's end, lies much that is unsaid, and Godwin makes clear that both her characters are equally aware of all the silence contains.

This discussion of the obligation to recognize the dignity in each person's unique self comes after Lily's visit to Theo's grave, where she finds that someone, most likely the Mullinses, has preceded her. Lily's tribute of a perfect rose in a tasteful bud vase must compete with the garish spectacle of hideously colored plastic lilies in an equally hideous green pot. Sickened by the gift and the suspected givers, Lily nonetheless must acknowledge the good intentions that lie behind the offering. As she contemplates the artificial flowers, she thinks: "Of course, they had meant well; the awful thing had probably cost a lot more money than her two roses. And it was only she, not they, who had seen the irony of the odious flowers just happening to represent the ones she shared a name with. They hadn't thought them odious; they had thought them beautiful" (*ASF,* 521).

These incidents and these observations indicate that on this second climb Lily is coming closer to the dying to oneself without dying that she envisions on the earlier, aborted climb up the hill to her house. In terms of fiction, she is becoming more in tune with perspectives other than her own, imagining how the Mullinses or whoever must have felt about the flowers and realizing that those feelings and her own very different ones are equally true. In terms of fiction, her attitude about the uniqueness and sacredness of each individual's personality is the attitude that has led Godwin to the use of multiple perspectives in *A Southern Family,* allowing Snow Mullins, for instance, to tell her own story rather than filtering it through the ironic slant of a more typical Godwin narrator-character.

When Lily and Sister Patrick get around to discussing Jason, Lily tells the nun about Jason's current life, shuttled back and forth between Granny Squirrel and his weekends with Lily and Ralph and about the child's uncanny ability to maintain himself despite the vast differences in those two worlds. When she gives Sister Patrick some details about the Mullinses' encampment where Jason lives, the sister says, "It doesn't sound all bad. . . . He has so many people to love him, to teach him different things" (*ASF,*

531), and Lily has to agree. She even admits a shift in her attitudes about background and roots: "But 'roots' don't matter to me much anymore. Ancestors-in-common are just more antique clutter and old debris. I care about what's here for me to do *now*" (*ASF,* 532).

When Sister Patrick shyly confides to Lily a dream she has had about Theo the night before—a dream in which Theo wants to tell her something, leave a message with her, but can't because she is not wearing her hearing aids in the dream—Lily seizes on what the nun tells her and draws an important conclusion from the suggestion of the dream's images. That conclusion is as important for the novel as a whole as it is for the nun's dream and what that dream means to the mother who hears it. Lily tells Sister Patrick that

It was Theo's way of sending a message that it's all right. . . . The details of how he was . . . struck down, exactly what *happened* that day, well, they aren't important: they're just past history. . . . But in the realm that matters, the realm where the indestructible personality lives on, the realm mere history can't touch, Theo lives. He lives, and right now he is in the process of climbing that very steep hill to sanctity; he's on the way to wash his hands so that he'll be fit to—. . .—to shake hands with God. (*ASF,* 536)

On the anniversary of Theo's death, in what she perceives as a gift from Sister Patrick, Lily finds the way she needs to think about the death of her son. That way may not redeem the years of not acknowledging his nature or of not seeing him as he was and may not make Lily not guilty of the charges leveled at her by Snow. But the interpretation of Sister Patrick's dream allows both Lily and Godwin to resolve the dilemma that Julia's distinction between narrative and interpretation raises and that permeates the search for sense and truth and meaning in the lives of all the novel's characters. If one concentrates, as Lily has decided to do, on what one can do now and if one takes the messages of the present without holding them accountable for the details of the past, one can reach a workable interpretation and can move beyond the disjointed and limited narratives that have been possible to this point.

This interpretation and Lily's comfort in it, in fact, her joy, suggest, in addition to other things, that the surviving Quicks, if Lily is read as the Quickest of the lot, can do something that Theo was unable to do. Through a leap of faith, one that might be described as a version of Christian existentialism, they can find the pattern and the meaning that Theo challenged Julia about that night before his death. They can emerge on the other side of whatever darkness he faced, not perfected but significantly closer to that vision of the transcendent self that comes to Lily on the afternoon she tries to climb Quick's Hill after running out of gas.

As if to reaffirm the direction of Lily's growth and the novel's thematic statement on the role that stories play in shaping and hiding our true natures from ourselves and the world, Lily's interpretation of Sister Patrick's dream is followed by a brief story about the nun's childhood horse, Shadow, who is also a character in her dream about Theo. The sister tells Lily that Shadow was a very unusual horse, and when Lily inquires why she was so unusual, Sister Patrick tells the story of Shadow's odd birth and development.

When she was born, Shadow was a total surprise to Sister Patrick's father, who had not known that the mare who was her mother was pregnant. The mare rejected the filly, so she was raised as one of the family, sometimes patterning her behavior after the dogs who were family pets, sometimes after the children themselves. Of course, her size eventually became a threat to the children, and when Shadow jumped on Sister Patrick in play and knocked her down, she was sent away for a year to a man who trained her to be a horse.

On Shadow's return to the family, Sister Patrick assumed responsibility for the horse. Shadow became her horse, but she was a completely different being, nothing like her old self, and Sister Patrick always felt that she had been the cause of Shadow's transformation, even though she realized that the change was inevitable. No one ever felt the same around Shadow again.

Sister Patrick always loved the horse and felt very close to her. After being professed in Belgium, she came home to say goodbye to her family before leaving for America, a visit likely to be her last with them. At the train station, her father felt uncomfortable with the nun who had come home in place of his daughter. Sister Patrick too felt uncomfortable until she thought of Shadow. She said to her father, "Well . . . you see they've made a nun out of me, just like they made a horse out of Shadow" (*ASF,* 537). The joke broke the tension and made her last visit satisfying and comfortable for them all. The story and the joke also reemphasize the important lesson of allowing others their true nature, no matter what false and more acceptable, easier natures we may have been accustomed to thinking of as theirs.

Engaging with the Realities of the Larger World

Just as the multiple perspectives that comprise the narration of *A Southern Family* broaden the scope of the novel and just as each individual's perspective becomes broader, more inclusive and sympathetic, as the story unfolds, so does Godwin's treatment of larger social issues broaden in this novel. One criticism frequently leveled against women's fiction in general and Godwin's fiction specifically is that its intense focus on the personal—on the details of an individual life (usually the life of someone born to a relatively high station)—limits its broader significance. These writers are frequently accused of ignoring larger social issues as they scrutinize and analyze every iota of the personal issues confronting their characters.

Careful examination of Godwin's work demonstrates that such a criticism is not well founded. Although the emphasis of all her novels, including *A Southern Family,* is primarily on the personal, all of the novels touch larger social issues, and that emphasis becomes greater as her career progresses. In *The Perfectionists,* the novel that has the least connection to larger social issues of any Godwin has written, the question of the privileged tourist class versus the Majorcan natives who are their hosts, especially Majorcan women, is part of Dane's initial response to the island, and her awareness of the subtle differences in her socioeconomic position as opposed to Penelope's is an indication that even within a narrow segment of British society, one's social and economic standing can be a matter of some importance. In addition, the custody situation involving Robin in that novel raises larger issues regarding child welfare and children's rights that go beyond the Empsons' personal situation.

Glass People, with its extended treatment of Cameron's political and social theories, goes beyond the hint of social issues in *The Perfectionists,* and the specific attitudes Cameron holds regarding Crystal City and the entire counterculture movement of the early 1970s raise social questions that may be somewhat dated 15 years later but that were, at the time of the novel's publication, pertinent and significant.

The Odd Woman is, in some ways, much more personal a story than either of the novels that precedes it because the male figure is more removed from the scene, kept more offstage so to speak, so the focus on the central female figure is naturally closer. Even so, that novel introduces two social themes that are central to Godwin's fiction. One is the question of feminism itself. In the character of Gerta and particularly in the scenes at the end of the novel that take place in Gerta's apartment as she and her friends try to get out the next issue of *Feme Sole,* the political, social, and economic implications of the women's movement are treated more explicitly than they are anywhere else in Godwin's work. These ideas about feminism are picked up in *A Mother and Two Daughters,* especially as Lydia emerges from her sheltered life and develops her friendship with Renee, and in a quite different way in *The Finishing School* as Justin Stokes observes her mother, her aunt, and Ursula DeVane as role models. But the direct and explicit addressing of the issues is more predominant in *The Odd Woman*.

Also emerging for the first time in *The Odd Woman* is the question of race, a social theme that is considered particularly important in the work of southern writers. *A Mother and Two Daughters* and *A Southern Family* both deal much more seriously with the issue than does *The Odd Woman*, but Jane Clifford's agonizing over how to deal with grading her black student, Portia Prentiss, the daughter of parents handicapped even beyond their socioeconomic limits and the great hope of her family for a chance to move beyond those historical limitations, though treated with humor, suggests the seeds of racial guilt that are often considered a trademark of southern fiction.

Violet Clay presents several social themes as part of the fabric of its story, and those themes prefigure some of the concerns raised in *A Southern Family*. First of all, the marriage of Violet's parents and the two families' responses to it and to Violet once she is orphaned suggest important class distinctions much more clearly than those hinted at in the earlier work. Furthermore, the decay that is undermining the southern aristocracy symbolized by Violet's grandmother and the desperate attempts to save face and stay afloat that such people are willing to undertake hint at the deeper explorations of that issue to come in both *A Southern Family* and *A Mother and Two Daughters*. Finally, the story of Sam's early life, her abuse by her stepfather, her running away, her rape, and her single parenthood—all of which have a profound impact on Violet's "merely personal" struggle—are precursors of the terrible and unexplained violence against an innocent female (and her child) that is involved in the tragedy of Theo's death in *A Southern Family*.

In *A Mother and Two Daughters*, the novel that comes closest to *A Southern Family* in terms of scope and larger social ramifications, there is the pervasive conflict between what Godwin labels the Old Guard and New Guard, picking up on inevitable changes demonstrated in *Violet Clay*. The issues of feminism, explored in *The Odd Woman*, get a much fuller, richer treatment here as well, including the question of abortion, so often a litmus-test issue for feminists. In the characters of Renee, Calvin, Camilla, and Azalea the relationship between blacks and whites in the Deep South becomes an integral part of the novel. Also integral to the story are the larger issues of education and religion raised by Cate's and Marcus's careers and by Lydia's experiences as a college student in midlife.

At first glance, *The Finishing School* may appear to shrink the portion of the canvas devoted to larger issues. Race, feminism, the passing of the old social order, even education and religion, seem to be of minimal importance in this novel. In the depiction of the "perfect" 1950s suburb, however, with its paint-by-number conformity, of the corporate loyalty to IBM that seems to have superseded religion and family for so many of those in Lucas Meadows, and of the total helplessness of Louise Stokes, who 20 years later would be termed a displaced homemaker, *The Finishing School* makes its own contribution to the emerging social agenda that is part of the foundation of Godwin's canon. For in the subtle havoc this cookie-cutter mentality wreaks on the sensitive, the unusual, the highly individual, we have a clear foreshadowing of the important lesson the Quicks and those close to them can learn only in the hindsight that follows tragedy.

This brief cataloguing of social themes does not even count the clearly significant theme of art and its importance to society as well as to the individual artist, the central concern of both *Violet Clay* and *The Finishing School,* not to mention at least the primary subtext of *A Southern Family.* But even if one discounts this particular social theme as too esoteric, just as arts courses are often considered frills on the contemporary educational scene, it is hard to support the claim that Godwin is not concerned with larger social issues.

It is possible to demonstrate how that concern has evolved and how Godwin tends to work the larger social issues into her admittedly personal narratives by examining a single issue in a single novel: the theme of race as it is treated in *A Southern Family.* The strands of this theme appear in several important ways as the characters work toward the broader, more fluid perspectives that signal growth and progress in the plot of this complex novel.

In several places the relationship between blacks and whites in the contemporary South is treated with humor. One such case is the relationship between Julia's father, Neville Richardson, and his neighbor, Mrs. Evans, the wife of a black doctor. The Evanses move onto Mr. Richardson's street, which also happens to be the street where Miss Alicia Gallant lives. Julia is both amused and pleased as her father reports his evolving relationship with this highly civilized and quite accommodating neighbor. She notes that after meeting Mrs. Evans her old-fashioned father adopts the acceptable term "black," in referring to her, rather than the outdated "colored," "darky," "Negro," or worse he might have used previously. When Mr. Richardson breaks his leg and is house bound, his new neighbor takes to dropping by to check on him and winds up frequently sharing his nightly toddy.

In another humorously handled episode, a black man, one Robert Jones, has been banned from the library after being accused of looking up a white woman's dress in the stacks. When the Library Board, on which both Mr. Richardson and Lily Quick serve, must decide how to make a policy that will effectively prevent Robert Jones from using the library, Mr. Richardson notes, in reporting the decision to his daughter, that times have certainly changed. Once, Robert Jones would have been lynched instead of temporarily banned from using the library. Lily makes the point that sways the board toward a liberal decision, noting that she does not think it is in the board's realm of authority to deny the comforts of literature to anyone, even, she implies, to a black man who might be prone to looking up the dresses of white women.

The events immediately surrounding Theo's death provide several examples of how the relationship between blacks and whites has changed in the South. While Ralph attends to the legalities and the details at the hospital on the evening Theo dies, Lily finds herself being comforted by "This nice Negro orderly" who holds her hand and walks her up and down the hall while they pray together, using some of his prayers, some of hers (*ASF*, 82–83).

As often happens when a loved one dies, the survivors comfort each other with memories of happier times when the deceased was alive. One of the memories of Theo, sparked by Ralph's wanting to notify his friend LeRoy, a black man Theo met when they were both working on one of Ralph's crews, is of the time when Theo and LeRoy ran away from Mountain City and wound up at Clare's Iowa apartment. Clare recalls the incident at some length in her letter to Theo, with fondness and amusement at the odd pair who were her overnight houseguests. LeRoy is famous in the family for the bath he took, delaying the dinner Clare had prepared for them for almost an hour while he conscientiously waited for her faulty tub to drain so that he could wash out the ring his bath had left. After dinner, LeRoy slept on Clare's sofa with a leopard-skin wrap for cover. The next day when the two fugitives headed back to North Carolina, she gave Theo her L.L. Bean down jacket but could offer LeRoy, who was much larger, nothing except the leopard-skin wrap. So he went home looking like an African chieftain of sorts, a caricature of a traditional stereotype. Neither the friendship between the two young men nor the relative ease with which LeRoy blended into the visit to Clare would have been possible for southerners even 10 years earlier than they occur in the novel.

Miss Alicia Gallant tells Jason a story about an encounter with the racial issue that took place during her long-ago childhood, when the rules govern-

ing contact between the races were much stricter than they are in the lifetime
of Clare and Theo and Jason. Getting on a crowded bus as a young girl,
Miss Alicia found only two vacant seats in the front area—the white area.
One was nearer the front, meaning more clearly a white person's seat, but
the man in the adjoining seat, a white man, was dirty, smelly, grossly unat-
tractive. The other choice was in a no-man's land, an area toward the back
of the bus that shifted between blacks and whites as the passenger popula-
tion shifted. On the occasion Miss Alicia remembers so vividly, the vacant
seat in this area was next to a black passenger, a very clean, nice-smelling
colored man, according to her report. She chose this seat and refused to
move when the driver of the bus challenged that choice. Her father, on hearing of his daughter's actions, praised her and told her that if she would always make a similar choice, she would come out "smelling like a rose" every
single time (*ASF,* 119–20). The irony of the Gallants' almost always coming out smelling like a rose because they are the Gallants does not escape
even Ralph, who is clearly in awe of her Gallant-ness, but, even so, the impulse behind this anecdote is again to treat with humor the subtle and ongoing changes in relationships between blacks and whites in the South.

Two more fully developed and serious sections of the novel also address
this important theme. One involves Ralph and the other focuses on Lily. As
the bridge generation between the Alicia Gallants and their own freer-
thinking offspring, they are the crucial generation in the South's shift during the civil rights era; thus, the emphasis on them is appropriate and
important.

Both Ralph and Clare remember an incident from Ralph's childhood
involving a black cook who accompanied Ralph, his father, and a group of
his father's friends on a fishing trip in the North Carolina mountains. The
black man went along to cook for the white fishermen during their week-
long stay. On the return trip, it was a tradition to stop in one particularly
backward rural town and have the sheriff come out and help the men play a
cruel joke on the man who had served them all week. The sheriff said loud
enough for the cook to overhear that his county had had to pass a law to
protect Negroes. The law forbid their presence in the county, whose residents were, according to the sheriff, too uncontrollably violent toward
blacks to prevent their being shot and killed just for being there.

Before witnessing this trick, Ralph had seen the fishing trip as a real
turning point in his life. He remembers it as his first experience with having
"been treated like a friend and an equal by these men" (*ASF,* 149). But he is
appalled by the joke and even more by the irony of his father's singing "The
Old Rugged Cross" while the terrified cook cowered flat on the floor of the

truck's bed to keep from having his head blown off by citizens enraged by his illegal presence in their territory. When he thinks back on the fishing trip, he remembers that he "had felt like a piece of wood cracking down the middle. He was pretty sure there was no such law. . . . Yet if he admitted the men had been cruel and wrong . . . then he would have to acknowledge that his father was not a good man" (*ASF,* 152). Torn by what he had seen, Ralph, who was desperate for acceptance, finally sided with his father, making a joke about what the cook they would bring the next year might do.

This same incident comes to Clare's mind as she and Julia, leaving their luncheon in Granny Squirrel, drive through the gorge where the black cook had to lie flat on the floor to protect himself. She recounts Ralph's report of the joke for Julia, but she does not remember Ralph as condoning the actions of his father and his friends. In her account, Ralph uses the story to illustrate the great strides that have been made in relations between the races, in society as a whole and in Ralph himself. He is proud, according to Clare, of his own liberal views in that area.

She goes on to tell Julia about another incident that she remembers, one that Ralph has apparently forgotten because Clare questions him about it shortly after Theo's death when they are remembering Theo's relationship with LeRoy. When Clare was a child, she and Ralph got on a crowded bus. Ralph asked a black woman to move to the back, she refused, the driver interceded on Ralph's behalf, and the black woman left the bus rather than back down. The thing that stands out in Clare's memory is that Ralph yelled after the woman, calling her a "Black bitch" (*ASF,* 368) even though he was getting the seat he wanted.

The ironies of the similarity of this encounter to the one Miss Alicia Gallant reports and of the difference in the way Ralph handles it and the way Miss Alicia does, along with the additional irony of Ralph's using selective memory to block out the example that undercuts his sense of racial progress, indicate the complexity of the issue. Seemingly discrete episodes involving race are actually tightly woven into the fabric of southern life and are inextricable from questions of class and character in ways far too complicated to unravel in the space of two or three decades, the span of the modern civil rights era.

A more positive and finally more significant treatment of the evolving nature of black-white relationships in the South is conveyed in Godwin's treatment of the relationship between Lily Quick and her masseuse, Thalia Thompson. The massage room where they meet is called the "incubator for their delicate friendship" (*ASF,* 161), and when Lily comes for her first massage after Theo's death, Thalia says to her, "I want you to take everything out of that head of yours and hand it over to me for an hour," to which Lily responds "Gladly. Take it all, Thalia. Only be careful you don't get scalded from the acid or defiled by the pitch" (*ASF,* 161). This exchange indicates their roles and reveals that each is concerned for the other. Godwin goes on to describe a "teasing tone, bordering on a scold, that [Thalia] permitted herself to use on Lily" (*ASF,* 161), the tone an indication of progress. That Thalia *permits* herself to use it, and only in this private room, this incubator, suggests how far there is to go.

Through the course of the novel, Thalia and Lily grow closer and more intimate. They share an old jealousy of Sister Patrick, who taught and influenced, in their opinion perhaps unduly, both their daughters. They also share an interest in writing: Lily, once a writer herself, comes to address Thalia's adult-education writing class. Thalia's father is one of the old people Lily visits on her rounds. In short, their lives gradually become intertwined. On the anniversary of Theo's death, Lily calls Thalia to cancel her massage. They discuss the anniversary, Lily thanks Thalia for her birthday card, they reschedule the massage for the following day. Although they still meet primarily in the relationship of server and served, they are clearly friends, and Lily is unafraid to acknowledge the personal nature of their connection. This is perhaps not an ideal example of racial harmony and equality, but it is an example of what Lily can do now on this issue. What she can do is superior to what many of her generation and background can or will do.

In her letter to Theo, Clare reports on watching a 1984 Democratic debate of presidential candidates. Her commentary on that event is a good summary of how far southerners (and Americans in general) have come on the racial question. She writes: "I had already sent money to Gary Hart, but ended up being more impressed by Jesse Jackson, the only candidate at that table who talked in larger realities. . . . But maybe it's because he knows he can never win that he is the only one who can afford to speak in a language of bold ideals. The others have a chance; therefore, they must be cautious, compromising" (*ASF,* 376).

Assembling the Transformed Selves

Clare's letter to Theo is the climax of the novel. The two chapters that follow that letter are entitled "No Saints" and "Anniversary." The second of these is the account of how Sister Patrick and Lily spend the first anniversary of Theo's death, a scene that serves the classic function of denouement. In the chapter that precedes it, "No Saints," Godwin handles action that also

adheres to a classical structure as she brings all the living principals together
at a South Carolina beach resort to evaluate their redefined sense of family
some nine months after Theo's death.

It is during this beach stay that Clare begins the novel that so closely resembles *A Southern Family*. It is here that Clare's life apart from her family
intersects life with them because her lover, Felix, accompanies her to the
beach. It is here that the impact of the last year's events on Lily and Ralph's
tenuous relationship become most evident, that Snow's ability to keep the
Quicks off balance is reaffirmed, and that the ups and downs of healing in
Jason and Rafe become evident to the family as a whole. It is also during
the events in this chapter that Clare comes to see herself as a secondary character, a recognition that seems to indicate a dramatic shift in Godwin's fictional direction.

As Clare considers her new role, she is not dissatisfied with the way it
feels: "She had become a secondary character at last. It felt strange. It felt
like being old, or invisible, yet curiously free. Was that how mothers felt
when their daughters succeeded them as heroines in the continuing drama
of humankind? If so, Clare had managed to learn one more thing about
lives she had not actually lived herself" (*ASF*, 486). Clare's coming to see
herself as a secondary character inside this story still so concerned with
that deadly twin-embrace of family and region that she had hoped to get
beyond is a perfect example of how the fiction writer can meet a goal in a
manner very different from what she (or he) imagined to be the means to
the desired end. The end product of *A Southern Family* we must presume
is quite close to, if not an exact replica of, the book that Clare begins on
the South Carolina island. And *A Southern Family* is a book quite different from any Godwin had written before, although it retains many of the
themes, character types, plot concerns, and obsessions that mark the earlier work.

It is not a novel exclusively about three male characters, as the novel
Clare abandons was to be, but *A Southern Family* does have three major
male characters, all with sections devoted to their perspective in Ralph,
Felix, and Rafe, not to mention the dead male, Theo, whose character and
actions generate the entire story. There is an independent woman, not quite
young perhaps, in Clare, but her professional success and the apparent solidity of her relationship with Felix suggest that she has already effectively
accomplished the escape from that deadly embrace that has so preoccupied
her predecessors. In writing Theo the long letter that serves as the novel's
climax, Clare in essence settles, as well as anyone ever can, the last haunting

questions about her relationship with family and region, and, as a by-product, she moves herself into the ranks of secondary characters.

The independent young women of *A Southern Family* are Snow Mullins and Felix's daughter, Lizzie, who appears briefly in an earlier passage but makes her main contribution to the story in the "No Saints" chapter. Snow clearly maintains her independence from the Quicks, and even living in the bosom of her clan in Granny Squirrel, she appears quite capable of independent thought and action. Lizzie, when she appears at the beach, quite unexpectedly, is also ready to declare her escape, to assert her independence. She has come to announce that she has fallen in love with and plans to marry an Orthodox Jew, that she has chosen a life of restraint and subservience to her husband, to culture and religion. Ironically, hers is a choice to place herself quite firmly in precisely that embrace that Godwin females usually struggle to escape. Her choice is sure to trouble her father, a nonpracticing Jew who will lament his daughter's willing sacrifice of intellectual and personal freedoms he cherishes.

Clare is the first person Lizzie tells about her plans, and it is Lizzie's story that makes Clare recognize her new status as secondary character and that enhances her awareness of her ability to know something about lives she has not lived. As she listens to Lizzie and filters what the girl is saying through her own experience, Clare decides how she wants to play her new role:

> Beginning to taste the dramatic possibilities in her role as secondary character, Clare decided to give Lizzie the first of her wedding presents, right now, in the car, before they joined the shoppers in Belk's. "If you want to know the truth," she said, speaking slowly not only for emphasis but because she never in her life expected to say such a thing, "I think I envy you. It's an experience I'll never have: giving myself away like that. When I was your age, I just couldn't afford to. I wanted . . . I guess I wanted to *keep* myself more than anything. And now I'm so solidly what I am, because of that early decision, that anybody who loves me would love me because I *am* that unmistakable single being. And I like it that way, I really do. But all the same, I envy you. It's an experience I once yearned for and it's an experience I would have liked to have." (*ASF*, 489–90)

This speech to Lizzie picks up on the differences in this younger woman and the sort of women Godwin has tended to write about before her. It also echoes *The Finishing School* with its emphasis on the necessity of yearning to combat the human tendency to congeal or, to use the term Clare uses here, to become solidly what one is. In *A Southern Family* Godwin enters a new stage of her career, one in which she *is* solidly what she is but in which she can use her imagination and keen observational powers to expand her perspective, shift her interests to other characters, and tap into their yearnings, their longings, in order to generate new art. That new art allows others their own natures without giving up the lessons of the typical Godwin woman's experience.

Lizzie proudly states her goal to Clare as looking "forward . . . to living a life where I no longer have to think of myself as the most important person in the world." Clare's external and internal responses to this announcement are quite different. Internally, she thinks, "You little dreamer," but externally "she kept her face straight as she delivered her line according to the script. 'That is a very noble ambition,' she told Felix's adored daughter solemnly" (*ASF*, 490). What this exchange reveals is a way of maintaining one's essential self without trying to interfere with another's essential nature. It also permits the shaping of life's stuff for the purposes of art, in that Clare can use Lizzie's yearnings to fuel her own imagination even as she recognizes her own solidity.

As Lily and Sister Patrick have their mountaintop chat on the anniversary of Theo's death—a mirroring of Julia and Clare's similar talk at the beginning of the novel before the death—Lily is working on a needlepoint pillow that will be her wedding gift to Lizzie, whom she meets for the first time at the beach. The pillow is based on a Paul Klee painting of a fish, but Lily is "adding her own embellishments" (*ASF*, 535). When Sister Patrick protests that her dream may be nothing more than her own mixed up jumblings, not a message about Theo and his death at all, Lily protests as she finishes up her needlepoint fish, persuading Sister Patrick to accept her view of the dream as an important message. Looking at her fish, she thinks, "Surely there was no such fish in nature. But that's why Klee was an artist. He trusted the nature of the inner eye. Which was, if you thought about it for a moment, *also* a part of nature" (*ASF*, 536).

Where to draw the line between art and reality has been an overriding concern of Godwin's fiction from the beginning. As *A Southern Family* unwinds, both its artist figure, Clare, and its consummate manipulator of real-life experience, Lily, appear to reach new conclusions about that distinction that fill them with confidence about facing the future. Clare has sometimes been frustrated by Julia's overweening sense of "Duty as an excuse to abandon [her] struggle for Self" (*ASF*, 56), but as she observes her friend, she sees that Julia's life "has supplied me with more than the material for a novel; it has illustrated to me that there are moral natures *outside* of books that are inherently superior to mine" (*ASF*, 57).

A Southern Family is full of such moments of recognition in Clare that signal a shift in Godwin's typical protagonist figure and in her approach to making fiction. The shift is toward a more expansive, more richly textured art that still manages to maintain the intensity and drama of the earlier work. Clare is still very much a Godwin woman. When Father Zachary comes to comfort the family on the evening of Theo's death, Clare notices the way in which he deals with people: "He makes himself available to people according to what they need, not what he thinks they *ought* to need," a recognition that fits perfectly with this new attitude, this new philosophy of the world according to Godwin. Clare realizes that the priest's approach to people is "not a bad lesson for a writer to learn"; then she feels "annoyed with herself for thinking of ways to improve her writing at such a time" (*ASF,* 90). The conjunction of these thoughts—the generous acknowledgment of the priest's strength, which she would do well to emulate, and the terrible selfishness of considering her work in the wake of real human tragedy—is a perfect metaphor for the path along which Godwin's work is likely to move forward.

Toward Moral Snooping

The cottage where the Quicks convene in "No Saints" (the chapter takes its name from the family's nickname for the cottage, which is full of ironies of its own) belongs to the Farquiers, a family of the old southern aristocracy, descendants of governors and senators. In the cottage are numerous family artifacts and remnants of their glorious past, and in the four years that Clare has been renting the cottage, she has searched through these artifacts, hoping to learn the "essentials" about "a certain kind of Southern family" through "studying the particulars," for, Clare believes, "once you [have] the essentials, you [can] grasp the typical" (*ASF,* 424–25).

Readers of Godwin's early work will recognize this tendency to snoop. Her female characters frequently read their husband's journals, search through lovers' wallets, seek any clue by any means in order to learn the essentials about someone, usually a man. The difference in these earlier snoops and Clare is that their goal was strictly personal. They wanted information that would help them figure out the man they were involved with—help them get him or leave him or make him align more closely with the ideal man they carry around in their heads. Clare snoops for a larger purpose. She wants to understand a culture, a society; she wants to draw conclusions that have implications beyond her personal life. She also seeks increased personal knowledge, wants to understand her own life better, but even her snooping suggests that she is perhaps more ready than she imagines to write a novel that truly deals with the fundamental issue scrawled across the folder that contains the novel she throws away after her brother's death: "Great social themes vs. obsessional private themes" (*ASF,* 385). Certainly, in *A Southern Family,* Clare's creator accomplishes that goal in a novel that is the fullest development, to date, of the fictional idiom that has become her trademark.

Notes and References

Chapter One

1. "The Uses of Autobiography," *The Writer*, March 1987, 22; hereafter cited in the text as "Uses."
2. "Journals: 1982–1987," *Antaeus*, Fall 1988, 186; hereafter cited in the text as "Journals."
3. Introduction to *Best American Short Stories 1985* (New York: Houghton Mifflin, 1985), xii; hereafter cited in the text as "Intro."
4. "Becoming a Writer," in *The Writer on Her Work*, ed. Janet Sternberg (New York: Norton, 1980), 237; hereafter cited in the text as "Becoming."
5. "My Mother, the Writer: Master of a Thousand Disguises," *New York Times Magazine*, 11 June 1989, 51; hereafter cited in the text as "Mother."
6. Jeanne Freeman, "Rearranging Things So They Make Sense," *Greenville* [South Carolina] *News*, 1 October 1986, 5B.
7. Mary Vespa, "A Vonnegut Protégée (and John Irving Pal)," *People*, 8 March 1982, 70; hereafter cited in the text.
8. "A Diarist on Diarists," *Antaeus*, Fall 1988, 12; hereafter cited in the text as "Diarist."
9. "How to Be the Heroine of Your Own Life," *Cosmopolitan*, March 1988, 194–97, 227; hereafter cited in the text as "Heroine."
10. "House Parties and Box Lunches: One Writer's Summer at Yaddo," *New York Times Book Review*, 10 August 1986, 3; hereafter cited in the text as "Yaddo."
11. Joyce Carol Oates, "A Bizarre Triangle Playing Out a Paranoid Tragedy," *New York Times Book Review*, 7 June 1970, 5.
12. Robert Scholes, Review of *The Perfectionists*, *Saturday Review*, 8 August 1970, 37–38; hereafter cited in the text.
13. Anatole Broyard, "The Fiction of Freedom," *New York Times*, 21 September 1972, L45.
14. Gene Lyons, review of *The Finishing School*, *Newsweek*, 25 February 1985, 87.
15. "Keeping Track," in *Adriadne's Thread: A Collection of Contemporary Women's Journals*, ed. Lyn Lifshin (New York: Harper & Row, 1982), 78; hereafter cited in the text as "Keeping."
16. St. Hilda's Press mission statement, in Longstreet Press catalog, Fall 1989, 15.
17. John F. Baker, "What Are Book Awards For?," *Publishers Weekly*, 18 December 1987, 9.

18. "Romancing the Shrink," *New York Times Book Review,* 12 October 1986, 14.

19. Mark Morrow, *Images of the Southern Writer* (Athens: University of Georgia Press, 1985), 34.

20. "Discovering the Form for Your Fiction," *The Writer,* December 1976, 14.

21. Joseph Barbato, "Breaking Out," *Publishers Weekly,* 31 May 1985, 33.

22. "Becoming the Characters in Your Novel," *The Writer,* June 1982, 12.

23. "The Southern Belle," *Ms.,* July 1975, 49.

24. "Godwin's Latest Novel Probes Young Person's Death," *Atlanta Journal-Constitution,* 6 December 1987, 13J.

Chapter Two

1. *Glass People* (New York: Knopf, 1972), 99; hereafter cited in the text as *GP.*

2. *The Perfectionists* (New York: Knopf, 1970), 17; hereafter cited in the text as *P.*

Chapter Three

1. *The Odd Woman* (New York: Knopf, 1974), 200; hereafter cited in the text as *OW.*

2. *Violet Clay* (New York: Knopf, 1978), 109–10; hereafter cited in the text as *VC.*

Chapter Four

1. *A Mother and Two Daughters* (New York: Viking, 1982), 191; hereafter cited in the text as *MTD.*

2. *The Finishing School* (New York: Viking, 1984), 15; hereafter cited in the text as *TFS.*

Chapter Five

1. *A Southern Family* (New York: Morrow, 1987), 91; hereafter cited in the text as *ASF.*

Selected Bibliography

PRIMARY WORKS

Novels

Father's Melancholy's Daughter. New York: Morrow, 1991.
The Finishing School. New York: Viking, 1984.
Glass People. New York: Knopf, 1972.
A Mother and Two Daughters. New York: Viking, 1982.
The Odd Woman. New York: Knopf, 1974.
The Perfectionists. New York: Harper & Row, 1970.
A Southern Family. New York: Morrow, 1987.
Violet Clay. New York: Knopf, 1978.

Short Story Collections

Dream Children. New York: Knopf, 1976.
Mr. Bedford and the Muses. New York: Viking, 1983.

Other

"About Pushcart Prize VIII." In *The Pushcart Prize VIII: The Best of the Small Presses,* edited by Bill Henderson, 11–15. New York: Avon, 1983.
"Becoming the Characters in Your Novel." *The Writer,* June 1982, 11–14.
"Becoming a Writer." In *The Writer on Her Work,* edited by Janet Sternburg, 231–55. New York: Norton, 1980.
"Being on Everybody's Side." *The Writer,* December 1979, 12–15.
"A Diarist on Diarists." *Antaeus,* Fall 1988, 9–15.
"Discovering the Form for Your Fiction." *The Writer,* December 1976, 11–14.
"House Parties and Box Lunches: One Writer's Summer at Yaddo." *New York Times Book Review,* 10 August 1986, 3.
"How I Write." *The Writer,* October 1987, 17–18.
"How to Be the Heroine of Your Own Life." *Cosmopolitan,* March 1988, 194–97, 227.
Introduction to *The Best American Short Stories 1985,* edited by Gail Godwin and Shannon Ravenel, xi–xix. New York: Houghton Mifflin, 1985.
"Journals: 1982–1987." *Antaeus,* Fall 1988, 186–95.
"Keeping Track." In *Ariadne's Thread: A Collection of Contemporary Women's Journals,* edited by Lyn Lifshin, 75–85. New York: Harper, 1982.

"My Mother, the Writer: Master of a Thousand Disguises." *New York Times Book Review,* 11 June 1989, 7, 50–51.

"A Novelist Sings a Different Tune." *New York Times Magazine,* 15 December 1985, 59, 62–63.

"One Woman Leads to Another." Review of *The Norton Anthology of Literature by Women: The Tradition in English,* edited by Sandra M. Gilbert and Susan Gubar. *New York Times Book Review,* 28 April 1985, 13–14.

"Romancing the Shrink." Review of *The Prince of Tides,* by Pat Conroy. *New York Times Book Review,* 12 October 1986, 14.

"The Southern Belle." *Ms.,* July 1975, 49–52, 84–85.

"Southern Men, Southern Lies." *Esquire,* February 1977, 126–29.

St. Hilda's Press mission statement. In Longstreet Press catalog, Fall 1989, 15.

"The Uses of Autobiography." *The Writer,* March 1987, 7–9, 22.

SECONDARY WORKS

Baker, John F. "What Are Book Awards For?" *Publishers Weekly,* 18 December 1987, 9. Quotes Godwin on the controversy surrounding the 1986 National Book Awards, which she judged.

Barbato, Joseph. "Breaking Out." *Publishers Weekly,* 31 May 1985, 30–33. Discusses Godwin's move from respected, midlist author at Knopf to best-selling novelist after her switch to Viking.

Broyard, Anatole. "The Fiction of Freedom." Review of *Glass People. New York Times,* 21 September 1972, L45. Praises the book as an expression of new fe male consciousness within a good novel.

————. "Miss Godwin's Gamut." Review of *Dream Children. New York Times,* 16 February 1976, L17. Strongly critical of Godwin's first collection of stories.

————. "See Jane Think. See Jane Love." Review of *The Odd Woman. New York Times,* 30 September 1974, L33. Criticizes the novel's heroine, her love affair, overwriting, underdramatization of key events, and length.

Crain, Jane Larkin. "Chronicles of Life on the Edge." Review of *Dream Children. New York Times Book Review,* 22 February 1976, 5, 22. Although she praises the conciseness of the stories and Godwin's ability to capture characters disconnected from themselves and their environment, she is critical of "a tedium and inconsequence that paralyze even her deftest effects."

Freeman, Jeanne. "Rearranging Things So They Make Sense." *Greenville* [South Carolina] *News,* 1 October 1986, 1B, 5B. Sheds light on some autobiographical connections in *The Odd Woman* and *A Mother and Two Daughters.*

Frye, Joanne S. "Narrating the Self: The Autonomous Heroine in Gail Godwin's *Violet Clay.*" *Contemporary Literature* 24 (Spring 1983):66–85. A strong and important article dealing with narrative technique in *Violet Clay;* it has significant implications for the other work as well.

"Gail Godwin's Latest Novel Probes Young Person's Death." *Atlanta Journal-Constitution,* 6 December 1987, 13J. Sheds light on autobiographical connections in *A Southern Family* and on Godwin's sense of the relatedness of the personal and the universal.

Gardiner, Judith K. " 'A Sorrowful Woman': Gail Godwin's Feminist Parable." *Studies in Short Fiction* 12 (Summer 1975):286–90. A valuable, if limited, reading of the short story in a feminist context.

Gaston, Karen C. " 'Beauty and the Beast' in Gail Godwin's *Glass People. Critique* 21 (1980):94–102. An interesting but flawed analogy is developed using the novel and the fairy tale ("Sleeping Beauty" as well plays a part in the argument). The feminist thesis distorts, to some extent, the novel's plot and resolution.

Gies, Judith. "Obligation, Fascination and Intrigue." Review of *Mr. Bedford and the Muses. New York Times Book Review,* 18 September 1983, 14, 37. Faults the shapeliness of the stories and "a problematic tone, chatty and oddly schoolmarmish"; especially critical of the tone in the "Author's Note"; prefers the novella to the stories, "A Cultural Exchange" to the other stories.

Hendin, Josephine. "Renovated Lives." Review of *A Mother and Two Daughters. New York Times Book Review,* 10 January 1982, 3, 14. Notes Godwin's interest in the tradition of American individualism as it relates specifically to female lives; although not entirely satisfied with the novel's tone, Hendin concludes that the novel is remarkable, "an expansive and imaginative celebration of American life."

Lehmann-Haupt, Christopher. Review of *A Mother and Two Daughters. New York Times,* 22 December 1981, C9. A laudatory examination of the novel, praising particularly the vividness of its lovable characters, its ingenious manner of offering and withholding information, and the sense of reality Godwin evokes.

————. Review of *Mr. Bedford and the Muses. New York Times,* 6 September 1983, C14. Praises the "classical and familiar" forms of the stories and the "culturally progressive attitudes" that underlie Godwin's vision.

Leonard, John. Review of *Violet Clay. New York Times,* 18 May 1978, C21. Finds the novel "too intelligent for its own good," saying that "You can't see the feelings for the ideas."

Lorsch, Susan E. "Gail Godwin's *The Odd Woman:* Literature and the Retreat from Life." *Critique* 20 (1978):21–32. Analyzes the novel's protagonist in terms of her using her literary interests as an escape from the realities of her life. Its failure to deal with Jane Clifford's tendency to create her own stories, a private literature, as a way, ultimately, to engage life, makes this article's argument only partially valid.

Lowry, Beverly. Review of *A Southern Family. New York Times Book Review,* 11 October 1987, 1, 28. Calls the novel Godwin's best.

Lyons, Gene. Review of *The Finishing School. Newsweek,* 25 February 1985, 87. Faults the author for her lack of a sense of humor and totally overlooks the narrative technique and the ironies involved in the story's telling; mistakes Ursula DeVane for the heroine, who is clearly Justin Stokes, the narrator.

MacLeod, Sheila. "Sisters and Lovers." Review of *The Finishing School. New Statesman,* 29 March 1985, 34. Astutely observes the crucial, to Godwin, connection between the shaping of art and the shaping of self and praises the narrative technique.

Mickelson, Anne Z. "Gail Godwin: Order and Accommodation." In *Reaching Out: Sensitivity and Order in Recent American Fiction by Women,* 68–86. Metuchen, N.J.: Scarecrow, 1979. Identifies with some accuracy the attitudes toward order in Godwin's work, primarily *The Odd Woman,* but then indicts those attitudes as inappropriate to contemporary females.

Morrow, Mark. *Images of the Southern Writer,* 34–35. Athens: University of Georgia Press, 1985. A brief, informal look at the author by a photographer who meets her while photographing her.

Oates, Joyce Carol. "A Bizarre Triangle Playing Out a Paranoid Tragedy." Review of *The Perfectionists. New York Times Book Review,* 7 June 1970, 5, 51. Important early praise for the deep psychological complexity of Godwin's work.

Pollitt, Katha. "Her Own Woman." Review of *Violet Clay. New York Times Book Review,* 21 May 1978, 10–11. Finds *Violet Clay* inferior to *The Odd Woman;* notes the importance of work, as opposed to romance, to plot but criticizes a lack of subtlety and a "general thinness."

Pritchard, William H. "Maiden Voyage." Review of *The Finishing School. New Republic,* 25 February 1985, 31–32. Praises Godwin's refusal "to overinvest in any single, 'true' point of view or nugget of meaning," a feat he credits to her style; finds the voice of the novel one that "one likes and trusts."

Renwick, Joyce. "An Interview with Gail Godwin." *The Writer,* October 1983, 15–17. Questions designed primarily to elicit responses of interests to other writers, but Godwin's comments on a shift from an intellectual viewpoint to one dominated more by direct observation and on her altered attitude toward writing from a male point of view have broader interest.

Rhodes, Carolyn. "Gail Godwin and the Ideal of Southern Womanhood." *Southern Quarterly* 21 (Summer 1983):55–66. Rather simplistic and limited readings of *The Odd Woman, Violet Clay,* and *A Mother and Two Daughters* in reference to Godwin's essay "The Southern Belle."

Scholes, Robert. Review of *The Perfectionists. Saturday Review,* 8 August 1970, 37–38. While admiring the extraordinary accomplishment of this first novel, Scholes criticizes it as being too feminine in its concerns to have universal appeal.

Smith, Marilynn J. "The Role of the South in the Novels of Gail Godwin." *Cri-*

tique 26 (1980):103–10. Deals with Godwin's protagonists' conflict between the impulse to flee the South and their need to hold onto certain southern ideals; argues that this conflict remains unresolved through *Violet Clay.*

Vespa, Mary. "A Vonnegut Protégée (and John Irving Pal) Warms a Bad Winter with a Hot and Ambitious Book." *People,* 8 March 1982, 69–70. Interesting in tracing the effect of best-seller superstardom on the author's career.

Wiehe, Janet. Review of *The Finishing School. Library Journal,* January 1985, 100. A brief but insightful review, important for its recognition of the link between life and art as shaped things.

Index

The Author

Jane Hill is senior editor at Longstreet Press in Atlanta. She received her Ph.D. from the University of Illinois in 1985 and has taught at Clemson University, the University of Illinois, and the University of Georgia. She is the editor of five anthologies of contemporary literature: *An American Christmas: A Sampler of Contemporary Stories and Poems, Street Songs 1* and *2: New Voices in Fiction, You Haven't to Deserve: A Gift to the Homeless,* and, with Emily Ellison, *Our Mutual Room: Modern Literary Portraits of the Opposite Sex.* She has published articles on James Dickey, Ann Beattie, Louise Erdrich, Michael Dorris, Christina Stead, Gail Godwin, and other contemporary fiction writers. Her stories and poems have appeared in *The Long Story, Kansas Quarterly, RE:AL, Quarterly West, Cream City Review, High Plains Literary Review, Emrys,* and other literary magazines. In 1989 she won the Frank O'Connor Prize for Fiction and is the recipient of fellowships from the Syvenna Foundation, Villa Montalvo, and the Georgia Council for the Arts.

The Editor

Warren French (Ph.D., University of Texas, Austin) retired from Indiana University in 1986 and is now an honorary professor associated with the Board of American Studies at the University College of Swansea, Wales. In 1985 Ohio University awarded him a Doctor of Humane Letters degree. The editor of the contemporary (1945–75) titles in Twayne's United States Authors Series, he has contributed volumes on Jack Kerouac, Frank Norris, John Steinbeck, and J. D. Salinger. His most recent publication for Twayne is *The San Francisco Poetry Renaissance, 1955–1960*.